RECIPES
of the
DEEP

**Complete Fish and Seafood Cookery
Microwave and Conventional Methods**

by
Terry Griffith

Take a child fishing today, and you won't have to get him off the hook later.

Copyright © 1982 by Terry Griffith

All rights reserved.

No part of this book may be reproduced or utilized in any form or by any means, electronic or mechanical, including photocopying or recording, or by any information and retrieval system, without permission in writing from the publisher.

International Standard Book Number
0-939114-56-9

Printed in the United States of America
WIMMER BROTHERS FINE PRINTING AND LITHOGRAHY
P.O. Box 18408
Memphis, Tennessee 38118

"Cookbooks of Distinction"™

ACKNOWLEDGMENTS

Thanks to the following people for recipes and for sampling.
Beatrice Griffith
Mona Griffith
Buck and Beth Hudson
Bill Nunnely
Walter Nunnely
Gary and Linda Oseman
Bubba and Mary Ann Pennel
Bill Shurtleff
Jim and Evelyn Stringer
Nina Jean Walker
Mike and Millie Young
U.S. Department of Commerce

Microwave recipes in this book were tested in a Sears Kenmore Microwave oven, model #99811 with 625 watts on HI. If your microwave has wattage lower than this, cooking time must be lengthened. If your microwave has wattage higher than this, cooking time must be shortened.

TABLE OF CONTENTS

TO CLEAN LOBSTER

1. Cook whole lobster. Place on back and cut in half lengthwise up to tail.

2. Cut away membrane with shears. Serve in shell or remove meat.

3. Remove and discard organs in body cavity.

4. Use lobster crackers to break claws away from the body. Remove meat inside.

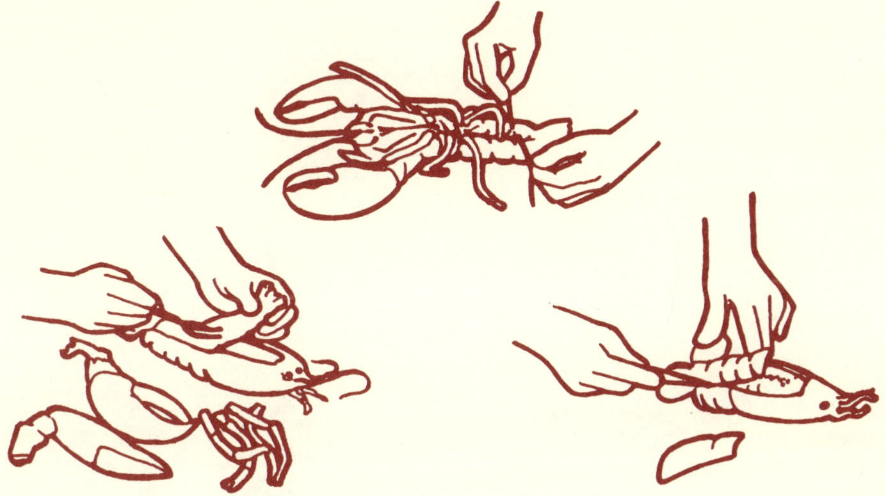

TO CLEAN SHRIMP

1. Hold shrimp in one hand. Carefully peel back shell from head to end. Remove shell.

2. Make slit along back of shrimp. Remove vein and discard.

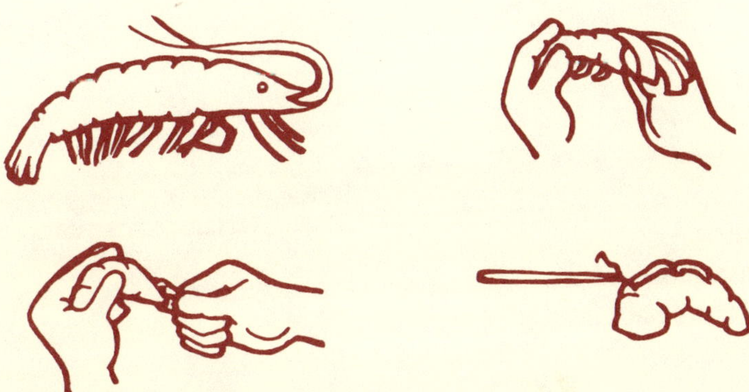

TO CLEAN CRAB

1. Grasp the flap and pull up and back. Discard and remove top shell.

2. Peel off "devil's fingers" and other body organs.

3. Remove claws and legs one at a time.

4. Remove the hard membrane to uncover the meat.

5. Crack large crab legs and remove meat.

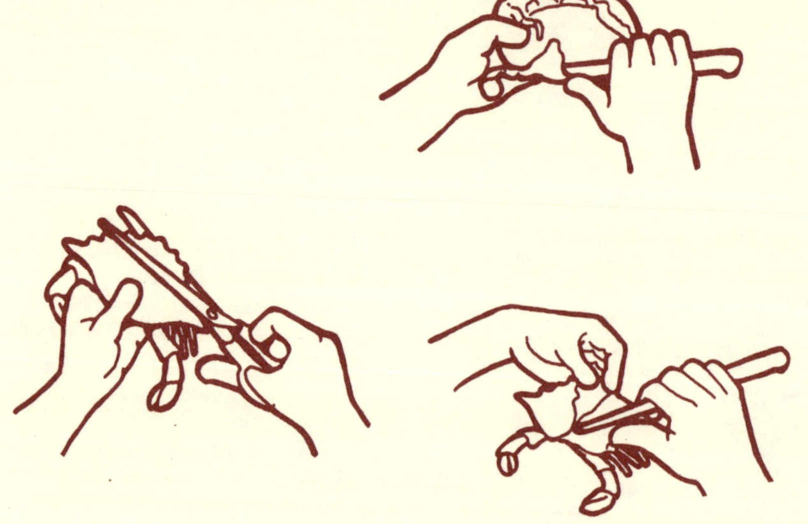

UTENSILS FOR THE FISH AND SEAFOOD KITCHEN

Scaler	Fish fryer
Oyster knife	Baking dish
Filleting knife	Pliers
Shears	Spoon
Clam opener	Thermometer
Clam knife	Timer
Fish poacher	Cleaver
Fish grill	Knife sharpener
Fillet fish grill	Skewers
Coiled steel pads	String
Heavy skillet	Baster
Dutch oven	Wide spatula

WINES TO SERVE WITH. . .

Appetizers . . .
Caviar—Dry sherry, chablis, champagne,
   sparkling rosé
Smoked salmon—Dry sherry, dry Madeira, champagne, sparkling
   wines
Oysters & shellfish—Chablis, Pinot Blanc, Pinot Chardonnay, dry
   graves, dry sherry, Green Hungarian

Soups . . .
Dry white wines—Pouilly-Fuisse, Chenin Blanc, Alsatians, Mosels
Semi-dry wine—Soave

Seafood Main Dishes . . .
All seafood dishes— Burgundian Chablis, Johannisberg Riesling,
   Folle Blanche, Schloss Johannisberg, Tramier
Grilled & poached fish—Muscadet, Alsatians, Soave, Pinot Blanc,
   Chardonnay, Chenin Blanc
Fish with strong spices & sauces—Gewurztramine, white
   burgundies, Cassis, Zinfandel, Pinot Chardonnay

TIPS ON BUYING FISH AND SEAFOOD

1. Fresh fish should have firm flesh.

2. Gills should be red or clear pink.

3. Avoid fish with a strong "fishy" odor.

4. Scales should be shiny and adhere tightly to the skin.

5. Scallops and shrimp should be firm and odor-free.

6. Eyes should be clear and bulging.

7. Clams, oysters, and mussels should be tightly closed and feel heavy.

8. Fish should be odorless.

SEASONINGS FOR FISH & SEAFOOD

Allspice	Poached or steamed fish & shellfish
Barbecue sauce	Broiled or grilled fish & shellfish
Basil	Add to lemon juice for easy sauce for broiled fish
Bay leaf	Add to poached or steamed liquid
Celery salt	Add to poached or steamed liquid
Cinnamon	Court bouillon
Cloves	Baked fish—sprinkle on fish before baking
Crab boil	Used with crab, shrimp or lobster for boiling, etc.
Curry powder	Broiled fish
Dill seed	Add to poached or steamed liquid
Ginger	Broiled and baked fish; sprinkle sparingly
Mace	Trout; scalloped fish; add to sauces & stews
Marjoram	Sprinkle in sauces or on broiled & baked fish
Mustard (dry)	Crab; broiled & baked fish; add to sauces & scalloped dishes
Nutmeg	Add to casseroles
Oregano	Good in chowders & stuffings; add with melted butter for shellfish sauce
Paprika	Use as garnish
Peppermint	Garnish for shrimp & scallops
Parsley	Use as garnish
Pickling spice	Sprinkle on broiled or baked fish
Rosemary	Salmon & halibut
Saffron	Halibut & sole
Savory	Crab & salmon; sprinkle on broiled or baked fish
Sage	Halibut & salmon
Thyme	Tuna, scallops, crab & sole; good in chowders & stuffings
Tarragon	All fish
Turmeric	Marinade for broiled salmon, lobster, shrimp

FISH COOKING GUIDE

COOKING METHOD	MARKET FORM	RECOMMENDED TEMP.	TIME*
Baked	whole, fillet, steaks, frozen	400	25 min.
Broiled	whole, fillet, steaks, frozen		15 min.
Charcoal grill	whole, fillet, steaks	medium	15 min.
Deep fat frying	whole, fillet, steaks, frozen	350	5 min.
Pan frying	whole, fillet, steaks, frozen	medium	10 min.
Flanked	whole, fillet steaks	350	8-10 min.
Poaching	whole, fillet, steaks	simmer	8 min.
Steaming	whole, fillet, steaks	boil	8 min.
Microwave	fillets, steaks, whole, breaded	HI	6 min.
Smoked	fillets, steaks, whole	150-175 200-250	1½ hr. 1½ hr.

Chart pertains to 2 pounds of fish.

LEAN FISH

Bass	Pompano
Brook trout	Salmon
Chub	Sea trout
Cod	Shark
Crappie	Skate
Cusk	Snork
Flounder	Sole
Fluke	Sunfish
Grouper	Swordfish
Haddock	Turbot
Mullet	Whitefish
Perch	

Lean fish can be frozen for up to 1 year.

FAT FISH

Barracuda	Pollack—salt water
Carp—fresh water	Porgy
Catfish—fresh water	Red snapper—salt water
Cod—salt water	Smelt—fresh water
Drum	Sheepshead
Eel	Striped bass—fresh water
Grunion	Sturgeon—fresh water
Hake	Ocean sunfish—salt water
Herring	
Pickerel	
Pike	

Fat fish can be frozen for 2-3 months.

APPETIZERS

SAUTÉED MUSHROOMS

1 pound mushrooms
2 teaspoons vegetable oil
1 tablespoon soy sauce

2 tablespoons water
1 teaspoon sugar
1 tablespoon cornstarch

Wash and slice mushrooms. Sauté mushrooms in oil for 3 minutes. Combine remaining ingredients and stir into mushrooms. Cook for 3 minutes or until sauce is clear.

MICROWAVE: Place thinly sliced mushrooms in 1½ quart casserole. Combine remaining ingredients and pour over mushrooms. Cover and micro-wave on HI for 4 minutes. Remove and serve. Serves 6.

CRAB N' CRACKERS

1 6½-ounce can crab, drained
  and flaked
½ cup celery, chopped
2 teaspoons prepared mustard

4 teaspoons sweet pickle,
  chopped
½ cup salad dressing
Cocktail crackers

Combine all ingredients except crackers in large bowl. Mix well. Spread on crackers and broil at 350 degrees for 3 minutes.

MICROWAVE: Mix as above. Spread on crackers. Place on micro-proof serving platter and microwave on HI for 45 seconds.

ROAST OYSTERS

36 oysters in shell

1 cup butter or margarine, melted

Wash oyster shells. Place oysters on grill 4 inches from hot coals. Roast for 15 minutes or until shells open. Serve in shells with melted butter.

MICROWAVE: Wash oyster shells. Place oysters in micro-pie plate 12 at a time. Cover dish tightly with plastic wrap. Microwave on HI for 10 minutes or until shells open. Repeat. Serve with melted butter. Serves 6.

OYSTERS MONIQUE

6 oysters on half-shell
2 tablespoons black caviar
1 tablespoon chives, minced

¾ tablespoon lemon juice
Sour cream

To each oyster, add ½ teaspoon caviar, sprinkle of chives, dash of lemon juice and scoop of sour cream.

SALMON ROLLS

½ pound sliced salmon, cooked
2 3-ounce packages cream cheese
½ teaspoon dry mustard

2 tablespoons dill pickles, chopped
½ cup parsley, minced
Lettuce
Lemon slices

Cut salmon into 3 inch long strips. Combine cheese, mustard and pickles. Mix well. Spread mixture over salmon. Roll strips and secure with toothpick. Dip each end of roll in parsley. Chill until firm. Serve on bed of lettuce. Garnish with lemon slices.

CLAM BAKE

3 dozen clams in shell
4 tablespoons parsley,
  chopped
2 tablespoons Parmesan cheese
¼ teaspoon pepper

¼ cup vegetable oil
4 tablespoons croutons,
  crushed
¼ teaspoon oregano
1 teaspoon paprika

Preheat oven to 250 degrees. Clean clam shells. Dry shells and place in skillet. Place in oven until shells open. Remove top shells wth clam knife. Place clams in half shell in large baking dish. Preheat oven again to 425 degrees. Combine parsley, cheese, pepper, and oregano. Sprinkle mixture on clams. Dab on vegetable oil, croutons, and paprika. Bake for 7 minutes. Remove and serve on toothpicks.

MICROWAVE: Clean clam shells. Dry and place 12 at a time on a micro-baking dish. Cover with vented plastic wrap and cook on HI for 4 minutes or until shells have opened. Place clams in half-shell in micro-baking dish. Combine parsley, cheese, pepper, and oregano. Sprinkle mixture over clams. Dab on vegetable oil, croutons, and paprika. Cook on HI for 2 minutes. Remove and serve. Serves 6.

CHEESE N' TROUT

2 pounds trout fillets
2 tablespoons onion, chopped
  finely
1½ teaspoons salt
¼ teaspoon pepper

2 tomatoes, chopped
¼ cup butter or margarine,
  melted
1 cup Swiss cheese, shredded

Place skinless fillets in greased casserole. Sprinkle with onion, salt, pepper, and tomatoes. Pour butter over fillets and broil 4 inches from heat for 10 minutes. Sprinkle with cheese and broil 3 additional minutes.

MICROWAVE: Place fillets in 1½-quart shallow microwave baking dish. Sprinkle with onion, salt, pepper, and tomatoes. Pour butter over fish. Cover and microwave for 8 minutes on HI. Sprinkle cheese over trout and let set for 2 minutes. Serves 4-6.

TROUT ROLLS

2 pounds trout fillets, skinned
2 tablespoons lemon juice
1 teaspoon salt
Cornbread stuffing (recipe
to follow)

2 tablespoons butter or
margarine, melted
⅛ teaspoon paprika

Preheat oven to 350 degrees. Cut fillets into 12 portions. Lay fish skinned side up and sprinkle with lemon juice and salt. Divide stuffing into ¼ cup portions. Place stuffing on fish. Roll fish around stuffing and secure with toothpicks. Place rolls, stuffing side up, into greased casserole. Pour butter over fish and sprinkle with paprika. Bake for 30 minutes or until tender.

MICROWAVE: Cut fillets into 12 portions. Lay fish skinned side up and sprinkle with lemon juice and salt. Divide stuffing into ¼ cup portions. Place stuffing on fish. Roll fish around stuffing and secure with a toothpick. Place rolls, stuffing side up, in greased micro-casserole. Pour butter over fish; sprinkle with paprika. Microwave on HI for 6 minutes. Serves 6.

CORNBREAD STUFFING
1½ cups soft cornbread crumbs
1½ cups soft bread crumbs
½ cup chopped celery
¼ cup chopped onion

2 tablespoons butter or
margarine, melted
2 eggs, beaten

Combine ingredients, blending well.

CRAB STUFFED AVOCADOS

2 avocados
2 cups crabmeat, cooked
1 tablepoon lime juice
1 tablespoon chili sauce

1 tablespoon Worcestershire
sauce
Lettuce leaves
4 olives, sliced

Chill avocados. Cut in half and depit. Chop crabmeat and toss with lime juice and sauces. Spoon into avocado halves and serve on bed of lettuce. Garnish with sliced olives. Serves 4.

SHRIMP-STUFFED EGGS

3 hard-boiled eggs
2 tablespoons shrimp, cooked
  & chopped
¼ cup mushrooms, chopped
1 tablespoon lemon juice
¼ teaspoon rosemary

¼ teaspoon thyme
⅛ teaspoon salt
⅛ teaspoon pepper
½ cup tomato juice
1 teaspoon parsley, chopped

Cut eggs in half lengthwise. Remove yolks and reserve. Cook mushrooms in water and lemon juice for 5 minutes and drain. Mix yolks, shrimp, mushrooms, and spices. Spoon mixture into egg whites. Place eggs in shallow casserole with tomato juice and cook at 350 degrees for 5 minutes. Garnish with parsley.

MICROWAVE: Cut eggs in half lengthwise. Remove yolks and reserve. Cook mushrooms on HI in water and lemon juice for 6 minutes and drain. Mix yolks, shrimp, mushrooms, and spices. Spoon mixture into egg whites. Place eggs in shallow micro-casserole with tomato juice. Microwave on HI for 2 minutes. Garnish with parsley. Serves 2.

ANTIPASTO

1 10-ounce can tuna
1 6-ounce jar artichoke hearts,
  chopped
1 6-ounce jar pimiento, chopped

1 cup celery, chopped
1 10-ounce jar green olives,
  chopped
2 tablespoons French dressing

Mix all ingredients except tuna. Refrigerate for 24 hours. Mix in tuna just before serving. Serve on crackers.

CRAB MORNAY

1 10¾-ounce can cream of
  chicken soup
⅓ cup white wine
1 pound crab meat, thawed
½ pound sharp cheddar cheese,
  grated

2 tablespoons butter or
  margarine
½ cup chopped onion
⅛ teaspoon Worcestershire
  sauce
1 egg, beaten

Mix together cream of chicken soup and white wine. Bring to a simmer. Add remaining ingredients. Cook at 275 degrees for 1 hour. Stir often. Remove and place in fondue pot. Serve with Triscuits or crackers. Serves 8-10.

Walter Nunnely

OYSTERS ON HALF-SHELL

4 dozen oysters, opened
2 pounds ice, crushed

½ cup Cocktail Sauce (page 33)

Place oysters in shell on bed of ice. Serve with cocktail sauce and garnish with mint sprigs. Serves 4.

SOUPS AND STEWS

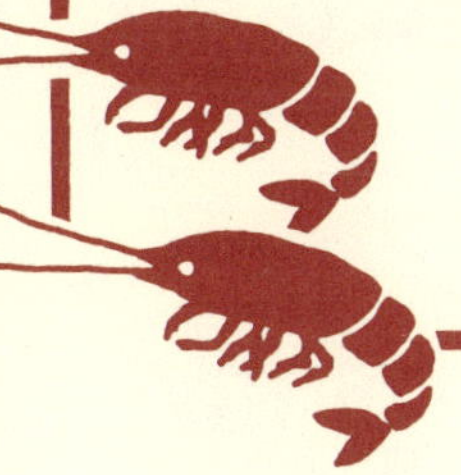

SHRIMP CURRY

½ pound shrimp, cleaned
    & cooked
½ tablespoon butter or
    margarine
1 saltine cracker

½ cup skim milk
½ teaspoon curry powder
⅛ teaspoon garlic powder
½ teaspoon salt
⅛ teaspoon pepper

Sauté shrimp in butter until pink. Remove from skillet and keep warm. Soak crumbled cracker in milk. Add shrimp and remaining ingredients. Place in casserole. Bake for 7 minutes at 350 degrees or until shrimp are golden.

MICROWAVE: Soak crumbled cracker in milk and set aside. In 2-quart micro-casserole, sauté shrimp in butter for 3 minutes or until pink. Add cracker-milk mixture to shrimp. Add remaining ingredients. Cover and microwave on HI for 3 minutes or until shrimp are golden. Serves 2.

OYSTER STEW

24 oysters or 1 pint
¼ cup butter or margarine,
    melted
1 quart milk

1½ teaspoons salt
⅛ teaspoon pepper
⅛ teaspoon paprika

Cook oysters in own liquid for 3 minutes until edges curl. Add remaining ingredients, except paprika. Bring to near boil. Sprinkle on paprika and serve.

MICROWAVE: Microwave oysters in own liquid on HI for 2 minutes until edges curl. Add remaining ingredients, except paprika. Microwave on HI for 3 minutes. Sprinkle with paprika and serve. Serves 4-6.

TROUT STEW

1 pound trout fillets, deboned
  and skinned
1 cup onion, chopped
2 tablespoons butter or
  margarine, melted
2 10¾-ounce cans cream of
  potato soup
2 cups milk

1 1-pound can tomato wedges,
  drained
1 10-ounce package frozen
  mixed vegetables
1 8-ounce can whole kernel corn
1 teaspoon salt
⅛ teaspoon pepper

Cut fillets into 1-inch cubes. Sauté onion in butter until clear. Add fish and remaining ingredients and simmer for 15 minutes.

MICROWAVE: Cut fillets into 1-inch cubes. Sauté onion in butter on HI for 5 minutes. Stir in tomato wedges, mixed vegetables, and corn. Cover and microwave on HI for 2 minutes. Add remaining ingredients. Cover and cook on HI for 7½ minutes. Let set for 4 minutes. Serves 6.

SHRIMP JAMBALAYA

1 pound shrimp, cleaned
  & cooked
1 onion, chopped
½ cup green pepper, chopped
¼ cup butter or margarine
2 tablespoons flour
1 cup rice, cooked

2 teaspoons salt
¼ teaspoon pepper
1 19-ounce can tomatoes
1 8-ounce can tomato sauce
⅛ teaspoon tabasco sauce
1½ cups water
1 cup ham, cooked and diced

Sauté onion and pepper in butter for 5 minutes. Blend in flour. Add remaining ingredients, except shrimp. Bring to a boil. Cover and simmer 30 minutes. Add shrimp and cook 10 minutes.

MICROWAVE: Mix flour and butter in a 4-cup micro-measure. Microwave on HI for 5 minutes. Add onion and green pepper. Sauté on HI for 3 minutes. Pour mixture into 3-quart micro-casserole. Add remaining ingredients. Cover and cook on HI for 10 minutes. Serves 4.

BASS CHOWDER

1 pound fish fillets
2 tablespoons bacon, cooked
   and chopped
½ cup onion, chopped
2½ cups potatoes, diced
1½ cups boiling water

1 teaspoon salt
¼ teaspoon pepper
2 cups milk
1 tablespoon butter or
   margarine
¼ cup parsley, chopped

Skin and debone fillets. Cut into 1-inch cubes. Fry bacon until crisp. Add onion and sauté until clear. Add potatoes, water, seasonings, and fish. Cover and simmer 30 minutes or until potatoes are soft. Add milk and butter and mix. Sprinkle with parsley and serve.

MICROWAVE: Skin and debone fillets. Cut into 1-inch cubes. Set aside. Microwave 3 slices of bacon on HI for 4 minutes. Remove and crumble. Add onions to bacon. Sauté on high for 2 minutes or until clear. Add potatoes, ¾ cup water, seasonings and fish. Cover and microwave on HI for 10 minutes. Stir often. Add milk, butter, and mix. Garnish with parsley and serve. Serves 6.

CRAYFISH GUMBO

½ cup tomatoes, stewed
½ cup celery, thinly sliced
½ cup green pepper, thinly
   sliced
½ cup onion, thinly sliced
1 tablespoon parsley, chopped

4 cups crayfish broth
2 cups crayfish, cooked
1 10-ounce package okra,
   chopped
½ cup rice, cooked
½ cup corn, cooked

Combine tomatoes, celery, green pepper, onion, and parsley. Place in saucepan and pour in broth. Simmer for 30 minutes. Add crayfish and okra. Simmer additional 10 minutes. Add rice and corn.

MICROWAVE: Combine tomatoes, celery, green pepper, onion, and parsley. Place in 1½-quart casserole and pour in broth. Cover and microwave on HI for 8 minutes. Add crayfish and okra. Microwave on HI for 2 minutes. Add rice and corn. Let set for 5 minutes. Serves 6.

SEAFOOD GUMBO SUPREME

1 pound pompano
½ pound shrimp, cleaned & deveined
¼ pint oysters
½ cup blue crab meat
2 tablespoons butter or margarine
2 tablespoons flour
¼ cup butter or margarine
1 cup green pepper, chopped

1 cup onion, chopped
1 cup celery, chopped
1 10-ounce can tomatoes, chopped, with juice
4 cups fish stock
½ teaspoon salt
½ teaspoon pepper
1 clove garlic, minced
1 teaspoon gumbo filé
Cooked rice

Cut fish, shrimp, and oysters into ¼-inch cubes. Prepare roux by melting 2 tablespoons butter in small skillet. Stir in flour over medium heat and cook until brown and smooth. Reserve roux. Add ¼ cup butter to 4-quart pot and sauté vegetables until tender. Add stock, salt, pepper, garlic and bring to a boil. Slowly add roux to vegetable mixture until well-blended. Simmer for 20 minutes. Add seafood and simmer an additional 20 minutes. Serve over cooked rice.

MICROWAVE: Cut fish, shrimp, and oysters into ¼-inch cubes. Prepare roux by blending butter and flour together. Cook on MEDIUM for 8 minutes or until smooth. Reserve roux. Add ¼ cup butter to 4-quart micro-casserole and sauté vegetables on HI for 3 minutes or until tender. Add stock, salt, pepper, garlic, and cook on HI for 2 minutes. Add roux to vegetables and mix well. Cook on medium for 3 minutes. Add seafood, cover, and cook on MEDIUM for 10 minutes. Serve over rice. Serves 8.

SEAFOOD SOUP

1 7-ounce can tuna, drained and flaked
2 tablespoons instant minced onion
1 teaspoon parsley flakes

1 10¾-ounce can cream of celery soup
1 10¾-ounce can vegetable soup

Combine all ingredients in saucepan. Mix well. Simmer for 15 minutes.

MICROWAVE: Combine all ingredients in microwave casserole. Mix well. Microwave on HI for 5 minutes. Let stand for 2 minutes. Serves 4.

SALADS

SARDINE LUAU

3 4-ounce cans sardines,
  drained
2 4-ounce cans mushroom
  buttons, drained
1 cup marinade (recipe below)
6 lettuce leaves

2 cucumbers, peeled and sliced
1 bunch celery, cut into sticks
12 radishes, rose cut
4 tomatoes, wedges
1 green pepper, cut in rings

MARINADE

½ cup French dressing
¼ cup soy sauce
2 tablespoons wine vinegar
2 tablespoons water

1 clove garlic, crushed
¼ teaspoon powdered ginger
½ teaspoon pepper

To prepare marinade, combine all ingredients and mix well. Makes 1 cup.

Place sardines and mushrooms in large bowl. Pour marinade over and chill for 1 hour. Prepare vegetables and chill. Remove sardines and mushrooms and drain. Arrange all ingredients except marinade on lettuce leaves. Serves 6.

ROCKFISH SALAD

1½ pounds rockfish fillets
1 quart water, boiling
1 tablespoon salt
¼ cup salad dressing
2 tablespoons onion, chopped
2 tablespoons sweet pickle,
  chopped

1 tablespoon lemon juice
1 teaspoon salt
1 cup green cabbage, shredded
1 cup red cabbage, shredded
6 lettuce cups
2 lemons, wedged

Place fillets in boiling water. Add 1 tablespoon salt. Cover and simmer for 10 minutes. Drain. Remove skin and bones and flake. Combine salad dressing, onion, pickle, lemon juice, salt, and fish. Chill for 2 hours. Add cabbage and toss. Serve in lettuce cups and garnish with lemon wedges.

MICROWAVE: Dampen paper towel with water. Place fillets, thickest part to the outside, in shallow microwave dish. Cover with paper towel and microwave on HI for 10 minutes. Remove skin, debone, and flake as above. Mix and serve as above. Serves 6.

STRAWBERRY 7-UP SALAD

2 3-ounce packages strawberry
  Jello
2 cups boiling water
1 large can crushed pineapple
  (drain and reserve liquid)

1 cup strawberries, drained
2 cups miniature marshmallows
2 cups 7-Up, chilled

Dissolve Jello in boiling water and cool. Add 7-Up, pineapple, strawberries and marshmallows. Refrigerate until jelled.

TOPPING

2 tablespoons margarine
2 tablespoons flour
½ cup sugar

1 egg, well beaten
Pineapple juice (reserved
  from above)

Mix together all ingredients, place over low heat, and stir until thickened. When cooled completely, spread over Jello. On top of this spread 1 cup Cool Whip and sprinkle with chopped nuts. Serves 6.

TUNA-APPLE SALAD

2 7-ounce cans tuna
2 cups apples, diced
½ cup celery, chopped

½ cup salad dressing
¼ cup raisins
1 tablespoon lemon juice

Drain tuna. Break into medium-sized pieces. Mix together with other ingredients. Chill and serve over lettuce. Serves 4-6.

APRICOT SALAD

2 3-ounce packages apricot
  gelatin
2 cups boiling water
2 cups cold water

2 large bananas, sliced
1 #2 can crushed pineapple
  drained (reserve liquid)
2 cups miniature marshmallows

Prepare gelatin according to package directions and let partially congeal. Then add pineapple, bananas and marshmallows. Pour into 9 x 13-inch Pyrex dish and chill until set.

TOPPING
1 cup pineapple juice
1 egg, beaten
2 tablespoons margarine
½ cup sugar

2 tablespoons flour
1 8-ounce package cream
  cheese
1 4½-ounce carton Cool Whip

Cook pineapple juice, egg, margarine, sugar and flour until thick. Add cream cheese. When cooked, fold in Cool Whip. Spread on top of congealed gelatin mixture. Serves 4-6.

KIDNEY BEAN SALAD

1 16-ounce can red kidney
  beans, drained
2 hard-boiled eggs, chopped

¼ cup sweet pickle relish
Mayonnaise or salad dressing

Combine all ingredients with enough mayonnaise to moisten. Chill. Serves 4-6.

SALMON-FRUIT SALAD

2 cups salmon (cooked and
   drained)
1 cup pineapple chunks
1 cup celery, chopped
½ teaspoon salt

⅛ teaspoon pepper
1 tablespoon onion, chopped
1 tablespoon lemon juice
¾ cup salad dressing

Mix together all ingredients. Chill and serve. Serves 6.

EASY SLAW

1 head cabbage, grated
3 carrots, grated
¼ cup onion, chopped
1½ teaspoons salt

½ teaspoon pepper
2 teaspoons sugar
Mayonnaise

Mix all ingredients with enough mayonnaise to moisten. Refrigerate.
Serves 4-6.

HEAVENLY SALAD

1 8-ounce can mandarin
   oranges, drained
1 8-ounce can crushed
   pineapple, drained
1 medium jar maraschino
   cherries, drained

1 cup miniature marshmallows
1 #2 can angel flake coconut
1 8-ounce carton sour cream

Mix all ingredients well with sour cream. Refrigerate. Serves 4-6.

SUNSHINE SALAD

1 cup boiling water
1 3-ounce package lemon
 gelatin
1 cup pineapple juice
1 tablespoon lemon juice

¼ teaspoon salt
1 cup crushed pineapple
1 cup grated carrots
½ cup chopped celery
½ cup chopped pecans

Dissolve gelatin in boiling water. Add juices and salt. Chill to thicken slightly. Add carrots, pineapple, celery and nuts. Turn into individual molds and refrigerate. Serves 4-6.

LOBSTER-SHRIMP ASPIC

1½ cups chicken bouillon
2 bay leaves
1 tablespoon dill
½ teaspoon cayenne pepper
1 package unflavored gelatin

2⅓ cups cold water
1 cup boiled shrimp
2 hard-boiled eggs
2 cups lobster meat

Place chicken bouillon in 2 quart saucepan. Add bay leaves, dill and pepper. Simmer for 10 minutes. Pour gelatin into mixture and dissolve. Pour in cold water. Mix and chill until sauce is thick. Place shrimp in 1½ quart mold. Slice hard-boiled eggs and place them over shrimp. Pour one-half of mixture over shrimp and eggs. Chill until firm. Place celery and lobster meat over shrimp and eggs. Add remaining gelatin. Chill until firm. Serves 2.

TROUT SALAD

2 cups cooked trout
2 cups cooked potatoes,
 chopped
3 hard-boiled eggs, chopped
⅔ cup salad dressing
½ cup carrot, grated

2 tablespoons onion, chopped
2 tablespoons parsley, chopped
1 teaspoon salt
¼ teaspoon pepper
Salad greens

Combine all ingredients except salad greens. Mix well and chill. Serve over salad greens. Serves 6.

CUCUMBER SALAD

1 3-ounce package lime Jello
¾ cup hot water
1 small carton cottage cheese

1 medium cucumber, chopped
1 medium onion, chopped
1 cup mayonnaise

Mix Jello and mayonnaise with boiling water using portable mixer. Let congeal slightly and add other ingredients. Congeal. Serves 4-6.

STRAWBERRY SALAD

2 3-ounce packages strawberry
   Jello
2 cups hot water
2 3-ounce packages cream
   cheese

1 cup sliced strawberries
1 cup chopped pecans
1 cup Cool Whip

Dissolve Jello in hot water. Cook. Mash cream cheese and add strawberries and pecans. Fold into Jello. Chill until slightly thickened. Add Cool Whip and chill until firm. Serves 4-6.

TUNA SALAD

1 7-ounce can tuna, drained
2 hard-boiled eggs, chopped
½ cup sweet pickles, chopped
1 tablespoon sweet pickle juice

½ teaspoon salt
¼ teaspoon pepper
2 teaspoons sugar
½ cup mayonnaise

Combine all ingredients and chill. Serves 4-6.

SHRIMP-FRUIT SALAD

2 cups shrimp, cooked and
   peeled
1 20-ounce can pineapple
   chunks, drained

1 cup orange sections, drained
⅔ cup celery, sliced
⅓ cup French dressing
Endive

Mix together all ingredients. Chill and serve on endive. Serves 6.

POTATO SALAD

5 medium potatoes
2 hard-boiled eggs, chopped
2 tablespoons onion, chopped
½ cup sweet pickle, chopped

½ cup mayonnaise
1 teaspoon salt
½ teaspoon pepper

Boil potatoes in water about 20 minutes or until tender. Peel and cut into bite-size pieces. Add remaining ingredients. Mix well. Serve warm or chilled.

MICROWAVE: Peel potatoes. Cut into ½-inch cubes. Place in 4-quart micro-casserole. Add ¼ cup salted water. Cover and cook on HI for 10 minutes. Rotate dish half-way through. Add remaining ingredients and mix well. Serves 4.

SCALLOP SALAD

1½ pounds scallops
1 quart boiling water
2 tablespoons salt
1 16-ounce can green beans, drained
1 cup celery, sliced

¼ cup onion, chopped
¼ cup green pepper, chopped
1 tablespoon pimiento, chopped
⅔ cup marinade (see below)
Lettuce

Place scallops in boiling salt water. Cover; bring to a boil. Reduce heat and simmer for 4 minutes. Drain and cool scallops. Slice scallops and combine with remaining ingredients, except lettuce. Cover and chill for 2 hours. Drain and serve on lettuce leaves.

MICROWAVE: Dampen paper towel with water. Place scallops in shallow microwave dish. Salt and cover with paper towel. Microwave on HI for 8 minutes. Remove. Drain and cool. Slice and mix as above. Serves 6.

MARINADE

½ cup cider vinegar
1 tablespoon sugar
¼ teaspoon salt

¼ teaspoon pepper
¼ cup salad oil

Combine all ingredients and blend well. Makes ⅔ cup.

FRUIT SALAD DRESSING

½ cup sugar
1 tablespoon all-purpose flour
1 egg

3 tablespoons lemon juice
¾ cup pineapple juice

Mix all ingredients and pour in saucepan. Cook over low until mixture is thick and clear. Chill and serve.

MICROWAVE: Combine all ingredients. Place in micro-casserole. Microwave on MEDIUM for 6 minutes or until sauce is thick and clear. Chill and serve. Makes 1¼ cups.

VINEGAR COLE SLAW

1 cup sugar
1 cup vinegar
1 teaspoon celery seed
1 teaspoon turmeric
1 teaspoon white pepper

1 head cabbage, chopped
1 large bell pepper, chopped
2-3 carrots, chopped
1 onion, chopped
1 teaspoon salt

Boil sugar, vinegar, celery seed, turmeric, and pepper together for 5 minutes. While mixture is hot, pour over remaining ingredients. Store in covered container in refrigerator. Keeps well for days.

MICROWAVE: Combine sugar, vinegar, celery seed, turmeric, and pepper; place in micro-casserole. Microwave on HI for 3 minutes. Pour over remaining ingredients. Cover and refrigerate. Serves 2-4.

VEGETABLES

ZUCCHINI CASSEROLE

2 16-ounce cans zucchini
  with tomatoes
1 teaspoon oregano
1 teaspoon basil

1 teaspoon salt
½ teaspoon pepper
½ teaspoon garlic powder
½ cup Parmesan cheese

Stir all ingredients together and place in 1½ quart casserole dish. Top with Parmesan cheese. Bake at 350 degrees for 15 minutes.

MICROWAVE: In a 2 quart micro-casserole, combine all ingredients except cheese. Cover. Microwave on HI for 8 minutes. Sprinkle with cheese. Let set for 2 minutes, covered.

ENGLISH PEA CASSEROLE

1 16-ounce can LeSeur
  English peas
1 10¾-ounce can cream of
  celery soup
⅓ cup salad dressing
¼ cup onion, finely chopped

1 egg, boiled and chopped
½ cup cheese, grated
¼ teaspoon Tabasco sauce
½ teaspoon Worcestershire
  sauce

Preheat oven to 350 degrees. Mix together all ingredients. Pour into 1½ quart casserole and bake for 40 minutes.

MICROWAVE: Mix together all ingredients. Place in 1½ quart microwave casserole. Microwave on HI for 10 minutes.

BROILED PEACHES

4 peaches, pared, halved, pitted
2 teaspoons lemon juice

1½ tablespoons butter or
margarine, melted

Place peach halves in shallow casserole. Brush with lemon juice and butter. Broil 10 minutes; turn; repeat process and broil 5 additional minutes.

MICROWAVE: Place peach halves in shallow micro-casserole. Brush with lemon juice and butter. Microwave on HI for 3 minutes. Turn; repeat process. Microwave 2½ minutes. Serves 4.

BAKED APPLES SUPREME

4 apples, cored
4 tablespoons sugar

1 teaspoon cinnamon
4 teaspoons butter or margarine

Preheat oven to 400 degrees. Slit apple skins half-way down. Place in 2 quart baking dish. Mix sugar and cinnamon together and place 1 tablespoon of mixture in each apple. Dot 1 teaspoon butter on top of mixture. Pour ½ cup water around apples to prevent sticking. Bake uncovered for 50 minutes.

MICROWAVE: Prepare as above, except cover casserole and microwave on HI for 6 minutes. Serves 4.

FRIED APPLE RINGS

3 apples
4 tablespoons butter or
margarine

4 tablespoons brown sugar
1 tablespoon cinnamon

Core apples and slice ½-inch thick. Melt margarine in skillet. Add apple rings, sprinkle with brown sugar, and fry until brown.

MICROWAVE: Arrange slices on micro-baking dish. Dot with butter, sprinkle with brown sugar. Cook 4 minutes on HI. Allow to cool. Serves 6.

STUFFINGS, SAUCES AND DRESSINGS

VELOUTÉ SAUCE

2 tablespoons flour
2 tablespoons butter or
  margarine, melted

1 cup fish stock
¼ teaspoon salt
¼ teaspoon pepper

Combine flour and butter. Cook until light brown. Stir in 1 cup fish stock until sauce thickens. Add seasonings and simmer for 10 minutes.

MICROWAVE: Combine flour and butter in micro-dish. Cook on HI for 3 minutes. Stir in ¾ cup fish stock. Cook on HI for 3 minutes. Add seasonings. Cook on HI for 5 minutes. Makes 1 cup.

CAVIAR DIP

1 pint yogurt
¼ cup cream
1½ cups caviar
½ onion, chopped

1 teaspoon black pepper
1 teaspoon lemon juice
1 egg, hard-boiled and chopped

Mix all ingredients together. Sprinkle eggs on top. Serve with raw carrots, celery, and cauliflower.

HOLLANDAISE SAUCE

½ cup butter or margarine
3 egg yolks
2 tablespoons lemon juice

½ teaspoon salt
½ teaspoon dry mustard
¼ teaspoon cayenne pepper

Heat butter in saucepan until it melts. Beat egg yolks and lemon juice together. Add remaining ingredients. Mix well. Pour hot butter into mixture gradually until well blended. Serve warm.

MICROWAVE: Place butter in 2-cup dish and microwave on HI for 45 seconds. Add egg yolks, blend, and mix in remaining ingredients. Microwave on HI for 1 minute. Stir twice. Serve warm. Makes 1 cup.

REMOULADE SAUCE

1 cup salad dressing
1 tablespoon onion, chopped
1 tablespoon parsley, chopped
1 tablespoon celery, chopped
2 tablespoons mustard,
   prepared
1 tablespoon horseradish

½ teaspoon paprika
½ teaspoon salt
⅛ teaspoon Tabasco sauce
½ cup salad oil
1 teaspoon vinegar
½ teaspoon Worcestershire
   sauce

Combine all ingredients in glass dish. Refrigerate for 24 hours.

CAPER SAUCE

1 cup yogurt
2 tablespoons capers, chopped
1 tablespoon lemon juice
1 tablespoon parsley, chopped

2 teaspoons instant minced
   onion
1 teaspoon grated lemon rind
¼ teaspoon paprika

Combine all ingredients. Mix well and chill. Makes 1¼ cups. Good with fried fish.

TARTAR SAUCE

1 cup mayonnaise
2 tablespoons kosher dill pickle, finely chopped
2 tablespoons onion, finely chopped

2 tablespoons olives, finely chopped
1 teaspoon lemon juice
⅛ teaspoon pepper
¼ cup sour cream

Combine all ingredients. Mix well and chill. Makes 2 cups sauce.

TARTAR SAUCE II

½ cup mayonnaise
¼ cup sweet pickle relish

¼ teaspoon white pepper

Mix ingredients well. Chill and serve. Makes ¾ cup.

COCKTAIL SAUCE

1½ cups catsup
1 tablespoon lemon juice
1 tablespoon Worcestershire sauce
2 tablespoons horseradish

1½ teaspoons sugar
⅛ teaspoon Tabasco sauce
¼ teaspoon salt
¼ teaspoon black pepper

Combine all ingredients and chill. Makes 2 cups.

PINEAPPLE STUFFING

¼ cup butter or margarine
½ cup sugar
3 eggs

1 20-ounce can crushed
  pineapple, drained
5 slices white bread, cubed

Preheat oven to 350 degrees. Mix butter and sugar until creamed. Add eggs, one at a time, until mixed. Mix in pineapple and bread cubes. Pour into greased casserole and bake for 1 hour. Serve with favorite fish.

MICROWAVE: Mix as above. Pour mixture into micro-casserole and microwave on BAKE for 10 minutes. Serves 6.

FISH STOCK

1½ pounds fresh fish trimmings
  (heads, tail, bones, etc.)
1 quart water
½ cup onion, chopped
¼ cup celery with leaves,
  chopped

1 bay leaf
½ teaspoon salt
¼ teaspoon thyme
¼ teaspoon pepper

Place fish in 4-quart saucepan and add water. Bring to a slow boil and cook over moderate heat for 5 minutes. Add remaining ingredients and simmer for 35 minutes. Remove from heat and strain. Makes 1 quart. Will keep up to 3 days in refrigerator.

MICROWAVE: Place fish in 3-quart micro-casserole. Add 1½ pints water. Cover and microwave on HI for 5 minutes. Add remaining ingredients. Microwave on HI for 6 minutes. Remove and strain. Makes 1 quart. Will keep up to 3 days in refrigerator.

LOBSTER DIP

1 cup lobster meat, cooked
⅓ cup salad dressing
4 tablespoons dry sherry

¼ teaspoon salt
¼ teaspoon paprika

Mix together all ingredients. Serve on crackers.

EGG SAUCE

¼ cup butter or margarine,
  melted
2 tablespoons flour
¾ teaspoon dry mustard
½ teaspoon salt

⅛ teaspoon pepper
1¼ cups milk
2 eggs, hard-boiled, chopped
1 tablespoon parsley

Stir flour and seasonings into skillet with butter. Add milk and cook until thickened. Stir often. Add eggs and parsley. Mix well and serve.

MICROWAVE: In 4 cup measure, melt butter on HI for 1 minute. Stir in flour and seasonings. Add milk gradually. Cook on HI for 6 minutes. Stir every minute until thickened. Add eggs and parsley. Cook on HI for 1 minute. Makes 1½ cups.

LEMON-CAPER DRESSING

½ cup salad dressing
1 tablespoon capers, drained
1 tablespoon lemon juice
½ teaspoon prepared mustard

½ teaspoon Worcestershire
  sauce
Dash Tabasco sauce

Combine all ingredients. Chill and serve. Makes ⅔ cup.

ORANGE-HONEY SALAD DRESSING

¼ cup orange juice, frozen
  concentrate
¼ cup honey
1 tablespoon vinegar

½ teaspoon dry mustard
½ teaspoon salt
⅔ cup salad oil

Mix together all ingredients except salad oil and beat. Add oil gradually while beating. Chill and serve. Makes 1¼ cups.

SEAFOOD BUTTER

Melt butter over low heat. Allow to cool. Skim foam from top. Pour off remaining liquid through strainer.

MICROWAVE: Place butter in micro-measuring cup. Melt on HI for 2 minutes. Allow to cool. Skim foam from top. Pour off remaining liquid through strainer.

Use as garnish for all seafood.

MORNAY SAUCE

½ cup Gruyere cheese, grated
1½ cups Veloute Sauce
   (see page 31)

½ cup heavy cream
¼ teaspoon salt
⅛ teaspoon cayenne pepper

Stir cheese into Velouté sauce. Add cream and seasonings. Heat until cheese is melted.

MICROWAVE: Mix as directed above. Melt in micro-dish on HI for 1 minute.

SUPREME SAUCE

Combine equal parts Hollandaise Sauce (page 32) and whipping cream. Mix well. Serve over your favorite white flaked fish.

BREADS

PECAN-RAISIN MUFFINS

1½ cups all-purpose flour
¾ cup sugar
¼ cup pecans
¼ cup raisins
2 teaspoons baking powder

½ teaspoon salt
1 egg, beaten
½ cup milk
¼ cup shortening, melted

Preheat oven to 400 degrees. Combine first 6 ingredients in bowl. Mix well. In separate bowl, combine egg, milk, and shortening. Make well in center of dry ingredients. Pour liquid in and stir until mixed. Fill paper muffin cups ⅔ full and place in muffin tin. Bake for 20 minutes.

MICROWAVE: Mix as above, except reduce baking powder to 1½ teaspoons. Fill paper muffin cups ½ full and place in microwave muffin tray. Microwave at 50 for 3 minutes. Set on HI and microwave for 1½ minutes. Makes 10-12 muffins.

ONION BREAD

1 egg, beaten
½ cup sour cream
1 tablespoon minced onion
¼ teaspoon salt

½ cup milk
2 cups Bisquick
1 tablespoon parsley

Combine egg, cream, onion, and salt. Mix well. Reserve ⅓ cup of mixture. Stir milk into remaining mixture. Add Bisquick and parsley. Blend well. Pour batter into 8½ x 4½ x 2½-inch loaf pan. Spread reserved batter over top. Baked at 350 degrees for 40 minutes.

MEXICAN HUSH PUPPIES

1½ cups corn meal
½ cup all-purpose flour
2½ teaspoons baking powder
1½ teaspoons salt
½ teaspoon pepper
⅓ cup onion, chopped

1 cup milk
1 egg, beaten
3 tablespoons vegetable oil
¼ cup Jalapeño peppers, finely chopped

Combine dry ingredients. Add remaining ingredients and stir until blended. Use a fork and drop heaping portions of the mix into hot, deep fat. Fry each hush puppy for 3 minutes or until golden brown. Drain on paper towels. Makes 30 hush puppies.

BANANA NUT BREAD

1¾ cups all-purpose flour
1½ teaspoons baking powder
½ teaspoon baking soda
½ teaspoon salt
1 cup mashed bananas
1 tablespoon lemon juice

½ cup butter or margarine, melted
¾ cup sugar
2 eggs
⅓ cup milk
½ cup pecans

CONVENTIONAL: Mix as below and bake at 350 degrees for 1 hour.

MICROWAVE: Place flour, baking powder, soda, and salt in large bowl and mix. Set aside. Pour lemon juice over mashed bananas. Add butter, sugar, eggs, and milk. Mix thoroughly. Blend butter mixture and banana mixture together. Make well in flour mixture and pour liquid in center. Mix flour in gradually. Pour into micro-Bundt pan. Microwave on MEDIUM for 9 minutes. Microwave on HI for 5 minutes. Let set for 4 minutes. Serves 8-10.

LIGHT MUFFINS

¼ cup sugar
¼ cup shortening
1 egg

1¾ cups self-rising flour
1 cup milk

Mix sugar and shortening thoroughly. Blend in egg. Add milk slowly and blend. Fill greased muffin tins ⅔ full. Bake at 350 degrees for 20 minutes. Makes 14 muffins.

FRESHWATER FISH

BASS BOUILLABAISSE

1 pound bass steaks
½ pint oysters
½ pound shrimp, peeled and deveined
¼ cup butter or margarine, melted
½ cup onion, chopped
½ cup celery, chopped

1 clove garlic, chopped
1¼ teaspoons salt
½ teaspoon pepper
1 bay leaf
¼ teaspoon thyme
1 1¼-pound can tomatoes
1 cup fish stock
¼ teaspoon saffron

Remove skin and bones from fish and cut into ½-inch cubes. Sauté onions, celery, and garlic in butter until tender. Add fish and remaining ingredients, except shrimp and oysters. Bring to a boil, then simmer for 10 minutes. Add shrimp and oysters and simmer an additional 10 minutes. Serve with French bread and sprinkle with Parmesan cheese.

MICROWAVE: Remove skin and bones from fish and cut into ½-inch cubes. Combine butter, onions, celery, and garlic. Microwave on HI for 3 minutes. Add fish and remaining ingredients, except shrimp or oysters. Cover and microwave on HI for 4 minutes. Microwave on LOW for 3 minutes. Add shrimp and oysters and microwave on LOW for 3 minutes. Serves 6.

OVEN-FRIED BASS FILLETS

2 pounds fish fillets
½ cup milk
1 teaspoon salt

1½ cups bread crumbs
¼ cup butter or margarine,
melted

Preheat oven to 500 degrees. Cut fillets into 6 serving portions. Mix milk and salt together. Dip fish into mixture and roll in bread crumbs. Place fish skin side down in baking dish. Baste with butter. Bake for 12 minutes or until fish flakes. Serves 6. Serve with beets in orange sauce, spinach salad, and rolls.

GRILLED BASS

1 4-pound bass
½ cup flour
1 tablespoon oil

½ teaspoon salt
¼ teaspoon pepper
⅓ cup butter

Cut fish so that it will lie flat when opened. Remove backbone. Rub on both sides with flour. Brush with oil. Sprinkle with salt and pepper. Rub one teaspoon of butter on each side. Place on grill. Baste often with remaining butter. Cook 8 minutes per side or until fish flakes.

POACHED BASS

4 bass fillets (approximately
2 pounds)
½ cup milk
½ cup sauterne
½ teaspoon salt

½ teaspoon pepper
½ teaspoon paprika
2 teaspoons butter or
margarine

Preheat oven to 350 degrees. Place fillets in well-buttered pan. Cover with ½ cup milk and wine. Sprinkle with salt, pepper, and paprika. Put ½ teaspoon margarine on each fillet. Bake for 30-45 minutes or until fish flakes.

MICROWAVE: Arrange fish in shallow micro-casserole. Sprinkle with salt and pepper. Pour wine and milk over fish. Marinate for 45 minutes. Turn fish once. Melt butter in micro-cup for 1 minute. Pour over fish. Microwave fish on HI for 10 minutes or until fish flakes. Rotate ½ turn after 5 minutes. Let stand 4 minutes before serving. Serves 4.

BASS BURGERS

6 ½-pound bass fillets
6 hamburger rolls
2 tablespoons butter or
margarine

⅓ cup chili sauce
6 cheese slices

Preheat oven to 400 degrees. Place fish in greased casserole. Bake for 15 minutes. Reduce heat to 350 degrees. Cut rolls in half, spread with margarine, and place bottom halves on casserole. Place one fillet on bottom half of roll. Top with 1 tablespoon chili sauce and slice of cheese. Cover with top half of roll. Bake an additional 10 minutes.

MICROWAVE: Place fish in micro-casserole and microwave on HI for 1 minute. Meanwhile, cut rolls in half, spread with butter and place bottom half of roll in casserole. Place one fish fillet on bottom half of roll. Top with 1 tablespoon chili sauce and slice of cheese. Cover with top half of roll. Microwave on HI for 2 minutes. Serves 6.

BROILED BASS STEAKS

6 ½-pound bass steaks
2 tablespoons butter or
margarine
2 tablespoons lemon juice

1 teaspoon salt
¼ teaspoon pepper
½ teaspoon paprika

Place steaks on baking pan. Mix remaining ingredients and pour over fish. Broil 4 inches from heat for 15 minutes or until fish flakes. Baste twice with sauce from pan.

MICROWAVE: Place steaks in micro-casserole. Combine butter, lemon juice, salt, pepper, and paprika. Microwave on HI for 2 minutes. Pour sauce over fish. Cover and microwave on HI for 6 minutes. Baste half-way through. Serves 6.

BAKED BASS

1 3-pound bass, pan-dressed
1 teaspoon salt
¼ teaspoon pepper

2 tablespoons butter or
margarine

Preheat oven to 350 degrees. Sprinkle fish inside with salt and pepper. Place on baking pan and brush with butter. Bake for 50 minutes or until fish flakes.

MICROWAVE: Sprinkle fish inside and out with salt and pepper. Place in micro-proof casserole. Brush with butter. Microwave on HI for 8 minutes or until fish flakes. Rotate dish every 2 minutes. Serves 4-6.

STUFFED BASS SUPREME

1 3-pound bass, whole and
cleaned
1 tablespoon butter or
margarine
½ cup onion, finely chopped
1 garlic clove, minced
1 tablespoon lemon juice

1 teaspoon salt
¼ teaspoon pepper
2 eggs, beaten
½ cup mushrooms, chopped
½ cup shrimp, shelled, deveined
and chopped
¼ cup parsley, minced

Wash and pat dry fish. Mix together remaining ingredients and lightly stuff into fish. Skewer and place in greased casserole. Cover and bake for 20 minutes at 400 degrees.

MICROWAVE: Wash fish and pat dry. Mix together remaining ingredients and stuff lightly into fish. Secure with toothpicks. Place fish in microwave baking dish.Cover head and tail with foil wrap. Cover with glass top. Cook on HI for 4 minutes or until fish flakes easily. Let stand for 4 minutes before serving. Serves 4-6.

PAN-FRIED BASS

3 pounds pan-dressed bass
¼ cup milk
1 egg, beaten
1 teaspoon salt
¼ teaspoon pepper
1½ cups bread crumbs
½ cup vegetable oil

Dip fish in mixture of milk, egg, salt, and pepper. Roll in bread crumbs. Pour oil in skillet and heat. Place fish in skillet and fry for 5 minutes per side until brown or until fish flakes easily. Drain on paper towels.

MICROWAVE: Dip fish in mixture of milk, egg, salt, and pepper. Roll in bread crumbs. Place fish in micro-casserole. Brush with 2 tablespoons oil. Cover and microwave on HI for 8 minutes or until fish flakes easily. Serves 6.

BIG BASS DINNER

16 medium-sized potatoes
2 cups salt
14 onions
10 pounds bass
Butter
Parsley
Lemon

Place potatoes and 8 quarts hot water in 12 quart kettle. Bring to boil. Add salt and onions. Cover and boil 25 minutes. Place fish steaks in basket and lower into boiling water. Boil 15 minutes. Remove fish and drain. Serve with potatoes and onions. Garnish with butter, lemon wedges and parsley. Serves 12-14.

BASS FONDUE

2 pounds bass
8 slices bacon

1 quart vegetable oil
1 teaspoon salt

Cut fish into bite-size pieces. Half fill fondue with oil. Add salt and heat to 375 degrees. Spear fish with fondue fork and cook until golden brown. Serve with sauce.

PAN-FRIED BREAM

2 pounds pan-dressed bream
½ teaspoon salt
¼ teaspoon pepper
1 egg

1 tablespoon milk
1 cup corn meal
2 cups vegetable oil

Sprinkle fish with salt and pepper. Beat egg lightly and blend in milk. Dip fish in egg mixture; then roll in corn meal. Place in skillet with hot oil. Fry until brown on both sides or until fish flakes. Drain on paper towels. Serves 4-6.

BLUEGILL BREAM

1 pound bluegill fillets
1 bottle beer

½ cup catsup
1 tablespoon horseradish sauce

Cut fillets into small pieces. Pour beer into saucepan and boil. Add fish and cook 4 minutes. Combine catsup and horseradish and serve with fish.

MICROWAVE: Cut fillets into small pieces. Pour beer into micro-casserole. Microwave on HI for 3 minutes. Add fish and microwave on HI for 3 minutes. Serve with sauce made by combining catsup and horseradish sauce. Serves 2.

CATFISH PARMESAN

6 ½-pound catfish,
   pan-dressed
½ cup tomato sauce
2 ¾-ounce packages cheese-
   garlic salad dressing mix

2 tablespoons butter or
   margarine, melted
2 tablespoons parsley, chopped
2 tablespoons Parmesan
   cheese, grated

Place fillets in greased 13 x 9 x 2-inch casserole. Combine remaining in-gredients, except cheese. Brush fish inside and out with sauce. Sprinkle cheese over. Let stand for 30 minutes. Bake at 350 degrees for 30 minutes. Just before removing from oven, turn setting to broil and place fish 4 inches from heat source for 2 minutes until crisp.

MICROWAVE: Place fillets in 13 x 9 x 2-inch casserole. Combine remaining ingredients, except cheese. Brush fish inside and out with sauce. Sprinkle over cheese. Let stand for 30 minutes. Microwave on HI for 15 minutes. Rotate dish after 7 minutes. Let stand for 3 minutes. Serves 6.

BAKED CATFISH

2 pounds catfish steaks
½ teaspoon salt
¼ teaspoon pepper
2 cups rice, cooked
2 tablespoons onion, grated
½ teaspoon curry powder

1 lemon, sliced
¼ cup butter or margarine
1 tablespoon parsley, chopped

Preheat oven to 350 degrees. Place steaks in greased 13 x 9 x 2-inch cas-serole dish. Sprinkle fish with salt and pepper. Combine rice, onion, and curry powder and spread over fish. Top with lemon slices and dot with butter. Cover and bake for 30 minutes. Remove cover to allow browning. Garnish with parsley.

MICROWAVE: Place steaks in 13 x 9 x 2-inch dish. Sprinkle with salt and pepper. Place butter in cup and microwave on HI for 1 minute. Blend in parsley, curry powder, rice, and onion. Spread over fish and top with lemon. Microwave on HI for 15 minutes. Rotate dish after 7 minutes. Serves 6.

BROILED SMOKEY CATFISH

6 ½-pound catfish, pan-dressed
⅓ cup soy sauce
3 tablespoons butter or
  margarine, melted
1 tablespoon liquid smoke

1 clove garlic, chopped
½ teaspoon ginger
½ teaspoon salt
1 lemon, wedges

Place fish in 13 x 9 x 2-inch casserole. Combine remaining ingredients except lemon wedges and mix well. Brush fish inside and out with sauce. Broil 3 inches from heat source for 6 minutes. Turn and broil for 6 minutes. Baste often with sauce. Garnish with lemon wedges.

MICROWAVE: Place fish on 13 x 9 x 2-inch micro-casserole. Combine remaining ingredients, except lemon wedges. Brush fish inside and out with sauce. Cover and cook on HI for 3 minutes or until fish flakes easily with a fork. Half-way through rotate dish ½ turn and baste with drippings. Garnish with lemon wedges. Serves 6.

ITALIAN CATFISH

1 cup onion, chopped
¼ cup butter or margarine
3 cups catfish, cooked and
  flaked
2 10½-ounce cans cream of
  mushroom soup
4 cups elbow macaroni, cooked

1 cup tomatoes, stewed
1 teaspoon salt
½ teaspoon oregano
¼ teaspoon pepper
1 teaspoon Tabasco sauce
2 tablespoons parsley, chopped
¼ cup Parmesan cheese, grated

Preheat oven to 350 degrees. Sauté onion in butter until tender. Combine with remaining ingredients, except cheese. Place in greased 3 quart casserole. Sprinkle with cheese. Bake for 30 minutes.

MICROWAVE: In a micro-proof 3 quart casserole, sauté onion in butter on HI for 3 minutes. Combine remaining ingredients except cheese. Cover and microwave on HI for 8 minutes. Add cheese. Let set for 3 minutes. Serves 6.

SOUTHERN CATFISH SPECIAL

**4 1-pound catfish, skinned and
  pan-dressed
½ cup French dressing**

**1 lemon, thinly sliced
¼ teaspoon paprika**

Preheat oven to 350 degrees. Brush fish inside and out with dressing. Cut lemon slices in half. Place 2 halves in each body cavity. Place fish in greased 14 x 9 x 2-inch casserole dish. Lay remaining lemon slices on fish. Brush with remaining dressing. Garnish with paprika. Bake for 35 minutes or until fish flakes easily with fork.

MICROWAVE: Brush fish inside and out with dressing. Cut lemon slices in half. Place 2 halves in each body cavity. Place fish in 14 x 9 x 2-inch micro-casserole. Brush with remaining dressing. Microwave on HI for 8 minutes or until fish flakes easily. Garnish with lemon and paprika. Serves 4.

FRENCH-STYLE CATFISH

**6 ½-pound catfish, pan-dressed
1 cup chablis wine
½ cup butter or margarine,
  melted
1 4-ounce can mushroom
  stems, drained
¼ cup green onions, chopped**

**2 tablespoons lemon juice
2 tablespoons parsley, chopped
2 teaspoons salt
¼ teaspoon bay leaves, crushed
¼ teaspoon pepper
¼ teaspoon thyme**

Place each fish on an 18 inch square of greased heavy duty aluminum foil. Combine remaining ingredients. Pour sauce over fish, using ⅓ cup of sauce per fish. Fold foil, using drug store wrap, around fish. Lay packages of fish on barbecue grill 6 inches from coals. Cook for 25 minutes. Roll foil back and serve. Serves 6.

FRIED CATFISH

**6 1-pound catfish, skinned and
  pan-dressed
2 teaspoons salt
¼ teaspoon pepper**

**2 eggs
2 tablespoons milk
2 cups corn meal**

Sprinkle fish inside and out with salt and pepper. Beat eggs and blend in with the milk. Dip fish in egg mixture and roll in corn meal. Place fish in skillet with ⅛ inch hot vegetable oil. Fry at 350 degrees. Brown on both sides. Drain on paper towels. Serves 6.

SUPREME CATFISH

**2 pounds catfish steaks
1½ cups flour, all-purpose
1 tablespoon salt
1 teaspoon pepper
1 teaspoon dry mustard
½ cup butter or margarine,
  melted
3 tablespoons lemon juice**

**1 teaspoon Worcestershire
  sauce
2 tablespoons soy sauce
2 teaspoons chives
1 2½-ounce jar mushroom
  buttons, drained
Parsley**

Wash and pat dry fish. Combine flour, salt, pepper and mustard and sift. Roll fish in mixture. Place fish in skillet with hot butter. Fry until both sides are browned. Remove fish and place on serving platter. Add lemon juice, Worcestershire sauce, soy sauce, chives and mushrooms to remaining margarine in skillet. Bring to a boil. Pour sauce over fish. Garnish with parsley. Serves 6.

BAKED CRAPPIE

4 pounds crappie fillets
1 teaspoon salt
¼ teaspoon pepper

¼ cup butter or margarine,
melted
3 slices bacon

Preheat oven to 350 degrees. Sprinkle fish with salt and pepper. Place on greased baking dish and brush with butter. Lay bacon slices over top of fish. Bake for 45 minutes or until fish flakes. Baste occasionally with drippings. Garnish with lemon wedges and parsley.

MICROWAVE: Sprinkle fish with salt and pepper. Place in greased, shallow micro-casserole. Brush with butter. Lay bacon slices over top of fish. Cover and cook on HI for 8 minutes, or until fish flakes. Baste with drippings every 2 minutes. Garnish with lemon wedges and parsley. Serves 4-6.

POACHED CRAPPIE

1 pound crappie,
pan-dressed

1 quart water
1½ tablespoons salt

Place fish in boiling salted water and simmer for 10 minutes or until fish flakes. Remove fish and serve with sauce.

MICROWAVE: Place fish in water and salt. Cook covered on HI for 4 minutes. Remove fish carefully and serve with your favorite sauce. Serves 2.

PERKY PERCH

2 pounds yellow-perch fillets
½ cup Caesar salad dressing
1 cup potato chips, crushed

½ cup Cheddar cheese,
shredded

Preheat oven to 500 degrees. Dip fillets in salad dressing. Lay skin side down in baking pan. Combine chips and cheese. Sprinkle over fillets. Bake for 15 minutes or until fish flakes easily.

MICROWAVE: Dip fillets in salad dressing. Lay skin side down in micro-casserole. Combine chips and cheese. Sprinkle over fillets. Microwave on HI for 4 minutes or until fish flakes easily. Serves 6.

STUFFED RAINBOW TROUT

2 8-ounce rainbow trout,
  pan-dressed
3 tablespoons butter or
  margarine
⅓ cup onion, finely chopped
⅓ cup apples, chopped
⅓ cup celery, chopped
⅓ cup carrots, finely chopped

⅓ cup croutons, crushed
1 teaspoon parsley flakes
⅓ teaspoon basil leaves,
  crushed
⅓ teaspoon salt
¼ teaspoon black pepper
¼ teaspoon Morton's Natures
  Seasonings

SAUCE

1 tablespoon butter or
  margarine, melted

1 teaspoon lemon juice

Sauté onion, apple, celery, carrots, and croutons in butter until soft. Add parsley, basil, salt, pepper, and seasonings. Mix well. Put ½ of stuffing in each trout and skewer. Baste with sauce. Place in casserole, cover and bake for 20 minutes at 400 degrees.

MICROWAVE: Combine 3 tablespoons butter, onion, apples, celery, and carrots in 1-quart casserole and microwave on HI for 3 minutes or until tender. Stir. Add croutons, parsley, salt, pepper, and seasonings and mix well. Place trout in 13 x 9 x 2-inch micro-dish. Put ½ stuffing in each trout and skewer. Baste with sauce. Cover and microwave on HI for 6 minutes or until fish flakes easily. Rotate half-way through.

BATTERED TROUT

2 pounds trout fillets
½ cup Caesar salad dressing

1 cup potato chips, crushed
½ cup Cheddar cheese, grated

Preheat oven to 500 degrees. Dip fillets in salad dressing. Place in casserole, skin side down. Mix together potato chips and cheese and sprinkle over fillets. Bake for 15 minutes or until fish flakes.

MICROWAVE: Dip fillets in salad dressing. Place in casserole skin side down. Mix together potato chips and cheese. Sprinkle over fish. Microwave for 6 minutes or until fish flakes easily. Half-way through, rotate ½ turn. Let set for 3 minutes. Garnish with lemon wedges. Serves 4-6.

BAKED TROUT

1 pound trout fillets	2 tablespoons butter
½ teaspoon salt	1 tomato, sliced
⅛ teaspoon pepper	½ green pepper, sliced
1 onion, sliced	1 tablespoon Worcestershire
⅓ cup chablis	sauce

Preheat oven to 450 degrees. Sprinkle trout with salt and pepper and place in casserole. Sauté onion in butter. Add wine, tomato, green pepper, and Worcestershire. Bring to a boil and pour over trout. Broil for 20 minutes. Garnish with paprika.

MICROWAVE: Arrange fish in micro-dish. Sprinkle with salt and pepper. Lay onion slices over fish and cover with wine. Marinate for 45 minutes. Turn fish once. Melt butter in microwave on HI for 2 minutes. Pour over fish. Add tomato and green pepper. Sprinkle Worcestershire over. Microwave on HI for 6 minutes. After 3 minutes, rotate ½ turn. Let stand 3 minutes. Garnish with paprika.

TROUT BROIL FANTASY

1 onion, chopped	3 lemons, quartered
½ cup butter	½ teaspoon salt
½ cup chablis	¼ teaspoon pepper
½ cup water	3 pounds trout fillets
⅛ teaspoon celery salt	¼ teaspoon paprika
¼ teaspoon garlic salt	

Preheat oven to 450 degrees. Sauté onion in butter. Add wine, water, celery salt, and garlic salt. Remove seeds from lemon and squeeze lemon juice into sauce along with lemon peel. Bring to a boil. Meanwhile salt and pepper trout and place in casserole. Pour sauce over. Place in oven and broil for 20 minutes. Garnish with paprika and lemon slices.

MICROWAVE: Arrange fish in micro-dish. Sprinkle with salt and pepper. Sprinkle onion over top and add wine, water, celery salt, and garlic salt. Squeeze lemon juice into sauce. Marinate fish for 45 minutes. Turn fish once. Melt butter for 2 minutes in microwave on HI. Pour over fish. Microwave for 5 minutes on HI. Let set for 5 minutes. Garnish with paprika. Serves 6.

TROUT AMANDINE

2 pounds trout fillets
¼ cup flour
1 teaspoon salt
1 teaspoon paprika
¼ cup butter or margarine,
  melted

¼ cup almonds, slivered
2 tablespoons lemon juice
4 drops Tabasco sauce
1 tablespoon parsley,
  chopped

Cut fillets into 6 portions. Combine flour, salt, and paprika. Roll fish in flour mixture and place skin side down in greased casserole. Sprinkle 2 tablespoons butter over fillets. Broil 4 inches from heat for 12 minutes or until fish flakes. Meanwhile, sauté almonds in remaining butter until golden. Remove and add lemon juice, Tabasco, and parsley. Pour sauce over trout and serve.

MICROWAVE: Place butter in 3-quart casserole. Cover and microwave on HI for 1 minute. Roll fish in flour. Arrange in casserole. Sprinkle with salt and paprika. Cover and cook on HI for 6 minutes. Rotate half-way through. Remove fish. Add almonds, lemon juice, and Tabasco to pan-drippings. Microwave on HI for 1 minute. Pour over fish. Serves 4-6.

SUPER BROILED TROUT

2 pounds trout fillets, skinned
2 tablespoons lemon juice
½ cup grated Parmesan cheese
¼ cup butter or margarine,
  melted

3 tablespoons shallots,
  chopped
¼ teaspoon salt
⅛ teaspoon Tabasco sauce

Place fillets in well-greased casserole. Brush with lemon juice. Let stand for 10 minutes. Add remaining ingredients. Broil 4 inches from heat source for 8 minutes. Spread cheese over fish. Return to broiler for 3 minutes.

MICROWAVE: Place fillets in well-greased micro-proof casserole. Brush with lemon juice. Let stand for 10 minutes. Add remaining ingredients. Cover and microwave on HI for 6 minutes. Spread cheese over. Microwave on HI for 2 minutes. Let set for 5 minutes. Serves 6.

SALTWATER FISH

COD MOUSSE

2 3-ounce packages
   unsweetened lime gelatin
1 cup boiling water
1 cup cooked cod, flaked

2 teaspoons onion juice
2 teaspoons lemon juice
2 tablespoons salad oil
1 teaspoon salt

Dissolve gelatin in water. Chill until slightly thickened. Combine remaining ingredients and fold into gelatin. Pour into two small molds and refrigerate until set. Remove from mold and place on bed of lettuce leaves. Serves 2.

COD N' WINE

1 pound cod steaks
3 shrimp, shelled
4 mushrooms
1 cup chablis

1/8 teaspoon Worcestershire
   sauce
1/8 teaspoon salt

Preheat oven to 400 degrees. Place fish in casserole. Clean and slice shrimp and mushrooms. Lay over fish. Combine wine, Worcestershire sauce, and spices. Pour sauce over fish. Cover and bake for 20 minutes.

MICROWAVE: Place fish in micro-casserole. Clean and slice shrimp and mushrooms. Combine shrimp, mushrooms, wine, Worcestershire, and spices. Microwave on HI for 2 minutes. Pour sauce over fish. Cover and microwave on HI for 3 minutes. Let set for 2 minutes. Serves 2.

ELEGANT CRAB

½ cup sherry
1 cup butter or margarine
2 cups celery, chopped
2 cups onion, chopped
2 cups green pepper,
  chopped

1 pound crab meat
2 10¾-ounce cans cream of
  tomato soup
2 10¾-ounce cans cream of
  mushroom soup
2 cups rice, cooked

Sauté celery, onion, and green pepper in butter until soft. Add sherry and crab meat. Mix well. Add tomato soup and mushroom soup. Let simmer for 7 minutes. Serve over rice.

MICROWAVE: In 2-quart micro-casserole, sauté celery, onion, and green pepper in butter on HI for 3 minutes or until soft. Add sherry, crab meat, tomato soup, and mushroom soup. Cook on HI for 3 minutes. Serve over rice. Serves 2.

CROAKER UNDER PRESSURE

2 pounds croaker, pan-dressed
¼ cup butter or margarine,
  melted
2 tablespoons lemon juice

1 teaspoon onion, grated
1 teaspoon paprika
1 teaspoon salt
¼ teaspoon pepper

Add water to pressure cooker. Place fish on steam rack. Mix together remaining ingredients. Pour sauce over fish. Cook for 30 minutes under 15 pounds pressure. Serves 4.

FRIED CROAKER

3 pounds croaker, pan-dressed
1 cup cornmeal
1 teaspoon salt
½ teaspoon pepper
1½ teaspoons paprika

½ teaspoon celery salt
¼ teaspoon onion powder
2 cups oil
Lemon wedges

Wash and dry fish. Combine dry ingredients and roll fish in mixture. Place fish in skillet with moderately hot oil and fry for 5 minutes on each side or until fish flakes. Drain on paper towel and garnish with lemon. Serves 6-8.

BLACK DRUM FILLETS

2 pounds drum fillets
⅓ cup barbecue sauce,
  hickory-flavored
¼ teaspoon salt
2 teaspoons frozen pineapple
  juice concentrate, thawed

1 tablespoon lemon juce
1 tablespoon onion, minced
3 tablespoons salad oil

Place fillets in greased baking dish. Combine remaining ingredients and pour sauce over fish. Broil 4 inches from heat for 12 minutes or until fish flakes easily. Baste with drippings occasionally.

MICROWAVE: Place fillets in micro-proof casserole and set aside. Combine remaining ingredients in separate casserole and microwave on HI for 2 minutes. Pour sauce over fish. Cover and microwave on HI for 3 minutes. Baste after 1½ minutes and rotate. Let set for 3 minutes. Serves 4-6.

FLOUNDER FINESE

1 1-pound flounder, skinned
  and deheaded
1 teaspoon salt
¼ teaspoon pepper

⅛ teaspoon Morton's Natures
  Seasonings
3 tablespoons flour
⅓ cup butter or margarine

Sprinkle fish with salt, pepper, and seasonings. Roll in flour. Place butter in shallow casserole dish with melted butter and bake for 15 minutes at 350 degrees. Serve with butter sauce.

MICROWAVE: Sprinkle fish with salt, pepper, and seasonings. Roll in flour. Place butter in shallow microwave dish. Microwave on HI for 2 minutes. Lay fish in dish and roll in butter. Microwave on HI fo 5 minutes or until fish flakes easily. Turn fish over half-way through. Cover and let stand for 3 minutes. Serve with butter sauce. Serves 2.

FLASHY FLOUNDER

2 pounds flounder fillets,
  skinned
2 tablespoons onion, grated
1½ teaspoons salt
⅛ teaspoon pepper

2 tomatoes, chopped
¼ cup butter or margarine,
  melted
1 cup Swiss cheese, shredded

Place fillets on greased baking dish. Sprinkle with onion, salt and pepper. Cover fillets with tomatoes. Pour butter over tomatoes. Broil 4 inches from heat for 12 minutes or until fish flakes. Remove from heat and sprinkle with cheese. Broil for an additional 2 minutes.

MICROWAVE: Place fillets in serving platter. In separate micro-casserole, place butter, onion, salt, pepper, and tomatoes. Microwave on HI for 3 minutes. Stir half-way through. Pour sauce over fish. Cover with wax paper. Microwave on HI for 3 minutes. Sprinkle with cheese and let set 2 minutes. Serves 6.

POACHED HALIBUT

1 pound halibut steaks
1½ cups hot water
1 teaspoon salt

1 teaspoon vinegar
2 teaspoons lemon juice
1 teaspoon butter or margarine

Place steaks in shallow pan. Add remaining ingredients and bring to a boil. Reduce heat to simmer and cook for 10 minutes or until fish flakes easily. Remove and serve.

MICROWAVE: Combine all ingredients except fish. Place in 8 x 12-inch micro-casserole and microwave on HI for 5 minutes. Carefully place steaks in water. Cover and microwave on HI for 2 minutes. Let stand 3 minutes. Serve with favorite sauce. Serves 4.

LOBSTER CASSEROLE

2 cups lobster meat, cooked
2 cups eggs, hard-boiled, chopped
1 cup salad dressing
2 tablespoons lemon juice
½ teaspoon Worcestershire sauce

3 tablespoons sherry
1 cup croutons, crushed and buttered
1 tablespoon parsley
1 tablespoon onion, grated
½ teaspoon dry mustard

Mix all ingredients together, saving ½ of croutons for topping. Put in greased casserole and top with remaining croutons. Refrigerate for 8 hours. Remove 1 hour before baking. Bake at 400 degrees 20 minutes.

MICROWAVE: Mix all ingredients together, saving ½ of croutons for topping. Place in greased 3-quart micro-casserole and top with remaining croutons. Refrigerate for 8 hours. Remove 1 hour before baking. Cook on HI for 6 minutes. Serves 4.

ESCALLOPED LOBSTER

1½ cups water
⅔ cup milk
3 tablespoons flour
1 teaspoon salt
⅛ teaspoon pepper
2 tablespoons celery flakes

½ teaspoon onion, minced
3 tablespoons butter or margarine
1½ cups lobster meat
2 tablespoons croutons, crushed and buttered

In top of double-boiler, place water, milk, flour, salt, pepper, celery, onion, and butter. Cook over hot water until sauce thickens. Add lobster meat. Spoon mixture into buttered ramékins. Sprinkle croutons over top. Bake at 350 degrees for 15 minutes. Garnish with parsley. Serves 4.

BROILED MACKAREL

4 1-pound mackarel   **Lemon slices**
2 teaspoons prepared mustard

Preheat oven to 450 degrees. Clean and dry mackarel. Slit down back and remove backbones. Spread inside and out with mustard. Place on broiler and brown on both sides. Garnish with lemon slices.

MICROWAVE: Clean and dry mackarel. Slit down back and remove backbones. Spread inside and out with mustard. Place in shallow micro-casserole and microwave on HI for 6 minutes. Sprinkle with paprika and cheese sauce. Garnish with lemon slice. Serves 4.

STUFFED MACKAREL

2 4-ounce mackarel,   **2 mushrooms, chopped**
** pan-dressed**   **2 green onions, chopped**
1 saltine cracker, crushed   **1 teaspoon parsley, chopped**
4 tablespoons milk   **½ teaspoon garlic salt**
4 raw shrimp, shelled   **¼ teaspoon salt**
** & chopped**   **⅛ teaspoon pepper**

Preheat oven to 400 degrees. Wipe and dry fish. Combine remaining ingredients and spoon into fish. Secure with toothpick. Place in casserole and bake for 20 minutes.

MICROWAVE: Wipe and dry fish. Combine remaining ingredients and spoon into fish. Secure with toothpicks. Place in shallow micro-casserole. Cover and microwave on HI for 5 minutes. Serves 2.

MIGHTY MACKAREL

1 2-pound mackarel
2 teaspoon prepared mustard
½ cup chablis
⅛ teaspoon Worcestershire
 sauce
¼ teaspoon salt
⅛ teaspoon pepper

⅛ teaspoon thyme
1 bay leaf
1 teaspoon green onion,
 chopped
1 garlic clove, minced
1 tablespoon parsley,
 chopped

Preheat oven to 350 degrees. Spread fish with mustard. Mix wine, Worcestershire sauce, salt, pepper, thyme, and bay leaf in casserole. Add mackarel and bake for 30 minutes. Baste often. Just before removing, sprinkle with onion, garlic, and parsley.

MICROWAVE: Spread fish with mustard. Mix wine, Worcestershire sauce, salt, pepper, thyme, and bay leaf in shallow micro-casserole. Add mackarel and microwave on HI for 8 minutes. Baste twice. Sprinkle with onion, garlic, and parsley and microwave on HI for 1 minute. Serves 4.

MACKAREL N' CHEESE

½ pound mackarel steaks
¼ teaspoon salt
⅛ teaspoon pepper
1 egg, beaten

1¼ cups milk
¼ cup sharp cheddar cheese,
 grated

Rub steaks with salt and pepper. Place in greased casserole and bake for 6 minutes at 350 degrees. Meanwhile, combine egg, milk, and cheese and mix well. Pour sauce over fish and bake an additional 6 minutes or until fish flakes.

MICROWAVE: Rub steaks with salt and pepper. Place in micro-casserole and cook on HI for 2 minutes 30 seconds. Combine egg, milk, and cheese and mix well. Pour sauce over fish. Cook an additional 6 minutes on HI or until fish flakes. Serves 2.

MAGNIFICENT MULLET

2 pounds mullet fillets, skinned
½ cup French dressng
1½ cups cheese crackers,
  crushed

2 tablespoons vegetable oil
¼ teaspoon paprika

Preheat oven to 500 degrees. Cut fillets into serving size pieces. Dip fish in dressing and roll in cracker crumbs. Place fish in greased baking dish and brush with oil. Bake for 12 minutes or until fish flakes. Sprinkle with paprika.

MICROWAVE: Cut fillets into serving pieces. Dip fish in dressing and roll in cracker crumbs. Arrange on microwave rack in micro-dish. Microwave on HI for 8 minutes or until fish flakes. Rotate dish ½ turn half-way through cooking. Sprinkle with paprika. Serves 4-6.

SUPREME OYSTER CASSEROLE

1 8-ounce can cream-style corn
½ pint oysters
1 egg
¼ cup milk

1 tablespoon butter or
  margarine
2 cups cracker crumbs

Preheat oven to 350 degrees. Combine corn, egg, milk, and butter. Layer corn, crackers, and oysters. Repeat. Cover with crackers. Bake for 35 minutes.

MICROWAVE: Combine corn, egg, milk, and butter. Layer corn, crackers, and oysters, Repeat. Cover with crackers and microwave on HI for 10 minutes. Serves 2.

DEEP-FRIED OYSTERS

24 oysters, about 1 pint
2 eggs, beaten
2 tablespoons milk
1 teaspoon salt

⅛ teaspoon pepper
1 cup crackers, finely
   crumbled
2 cups vegetable oil

Drain oysters. Combine eggs, milk and seasonings and mix well. Dip oysters in mixture and roll in crumbs. Repeat process. Fry in hot oil (375°) for 3 minutes or until golden brown. Drain on paper towels. Serves 4.

PAMPERED POLLOCK

1 pound pollock
1 teaspoon butter or margarine
1 tablespoon onion, chopped
2 teaspoons capers, drained
¼ teaspoon salt

⅛ teaspoon pepper
1 tablespoon lemon juice
¼ teaspoon thyme
1 tablespoon parsley,
   chopped

Preheat oven to 400 degrees. Place fish in greased casserole. Dot with butter. Cover with onions, capers, salt, pepper, and lemon juice. Bake for 20 minutes or until fish flakes easily. Sprinkle with thyme and parsley.

MICROWAVE: Place fish in shallow micro-casserole. Meanwhile place butter, onions, capers, salt, pepper, and lemon juice in 3-cup micro-container. Microwave on HI for 2 minutes. Remove and pour over fish. Cover and microwave on HI for 3 minutes. Let set for 2 minutes. Sprinkle with thyme and parsley. Serves 2.

FRIED REDFISH

2 pounds redfish fillets, skinned
1 cup buttermilk

1 cup Bisquick
2 teaspoons salt

Cut fillets into 6 portions. Place in shallow casserole. Pour buttermilk over fillets and let marinate for 30 minutes. Combine Bisquick and salt. Remove fillets and roll in biscuit mix. Fry for 10 minutes in moderate amount of oil until brown. Turn once. Drain on paper towel. Garnish with lemon wedge. Serve with malt vinegar. Serves 4-6.

SALMON LOAF I

1 16-ounce can salmon
½ cup milk
3 cups soft breadcrumbs
¼ cup butter or margarine,
  melted
⅓ cup salmon liquid
3 egg yolks, beaten

¼ cup green pepper, chopped
¼ cup onion, chopped
¼ cup celery, chopped
1 tablespoon lemon juice
⅛ teaspoon pepper
3 egg whites, beaten

Preheat oven to 350 degrees. Drain salmon; reserving liquid. Remove skin and bones and flake. Place milk in saucepan and heat. Add breadcrumbs and butter. Mix well. Add salmon liquid and beat until smooth. Add remaining ingredients, except egg whites. Mix well. Add egg whites. Pour into greased baking dish. Bake 45 minutes or until firm in center. Remove; let stand for 8 minutes. Remove from pan and slice.

MICROWAVE: Prepare loaf mixture as above. Then place loaf in microwave loaf pan. Microwave on HI for 9 minutes. Half-way through, rotate ½ turn. Let set for 5 minutes. Serves 6.

SALMON LOAF II

2 16-ounce cans salmon,
  drained & flaked
½ teaspoon salt
1 tablespoon pimiento,
  chopped

1 10¾-ounce can cream of
  mushroom soup
¼ cup butter or margarine,
  melted
3 slices white bread, cubed

Combine salmon and reserved juice with bread cubes. Add salt, pimiento, soup and butter. Mix well and place in greased loaf pan. Bake at 350 degrees for 45 minutes.

MICROWAVE: Mix together all ingredients. Pack into a greased 8 x 4 x 3-inch microwave loaf pan. Cover and cook on 70 (roast) for 25 minutes, or until center of loaf is done. Let stand for 5 minutes before serving. Slice and serve. Serves 4-6.

SALMONBURGERS

1 16-ounce can salmon
½ cup onion, chopped
¼ cup butter, melted
⅓ cup salmon liquid
⅓ cup dry bread crumbs
2 eggs, beaten
¼ cup parsley, chopped

1 teaspoon powdered mustard
½ teaspoon salt
½ cup dry bread crumbs
⅓ cup salad dressing
1 tablespoon sweet pickle, chopped
6 hamburger buns

Drain salmon, flake, and reserve liquid. Sauté onion in butter until tender. Add salmon liquid, crumbs, egg, parsley, mustard, salt, and salmon. Mix well. Shape into 6 burgers. Roll in bread crumbs. Broil 4 inches from heat for 3 minutes. Turn and cook and additional 3 minutes. Drain on paper towels. Combine salad dressing and pickle. Place burgers on bottom half of bun. Top with salad dressing mixture and cover with top of bun.

MICROWAVE: Prepare as above. Place shaped burger on buns; wrap in paper towels and microwave on HI for 3½ minutes. Combine salad dressing and pickle. Top burgers with spread and serve. Serves 6.

ALASKAN SALMON SANDWICH

1 16-ounce can salmon
1 cup salad dressing
2 tablespoons lemon juice
1½ teaspoons parsley flakes

⅛ teaspoon cayenne pepper
2 egg whites
6 tomato slices
6 slices white bread, toasted

Drain salmon. Remove skin and bones and flake. Combine salad dressing, lemon juice, parsley, and pepper. Beat egg whites until stiff. Fold salad dressing mixture into egg whites. Place a tomato slice on each piece of toast. Cover tomato with salmon. Place sandwich on baking sheet. Spoon salad dressing mixture over each sandwich. Broil 12 inches from heat for 8 minutes.

MICROWAVE: Prepare as above. Place sandwiches on micro-baking sheet. Spoon salad dressing mixture over each sandwich. Cover with paper towel. Microwave on HI for 2½-3 minutes. Serves 6.

SALMON N' EGG

1 onion, chopped
2 tablespoons butter or
  margarine
6 eggs, beaten

1 tablespoon milk
1 teaspoon dill
½ pound smoked salmon,
  sliced in strips

Sauté onions in butter until golden. Combine eggs, milk, and dill. Add salmon and pour into skillet with onion. Cook at 350 degrees until salmon flakes.

MICROWAVE: In 2-quart micro-casserole, sauté onion in butter until golden. Combine eggs, milk, and dill. Add salmon and pour into micro-casserole with onion. Cover and microwave on HI for 6 minutes, or until salmon flakes easily. Serves 4.

GRILLED SARDINES

12 fresh sardines
2 teaspoons powdered ginger
2 teaspoons lemon juice

½ teaspoon onion powder
2 teaspoons parsley, chopped

Preheat oven to 450 degrees. Place sardines on broiler and brown on each side. Combine sauce ingredients and pour over fish before serving.

MICROWAVE: Place sardines in shallow micro-casserole and microwave on HI for 4 minutes. Combine sauce ingredients and pour over fish before serving. Serves 2.

SCRUMPTIOUS SCROD

1 1½-pound scrod fillet
1 teaspoon salt
½ teaspoon pepper

1 egg, beaten
¾ cup crushed croutons
4 tablespoons vegetable oil

Preheat oven to 350 degrees. Cut fish into 4 serving pieces. Sprinkle with salt and pepper. Dip in egg mixture and roll in crumbs. Place in greased casserole. Cover and bake for 30 minutes or until fish flakes easily.

MICROWAVE: Cut fish into 4 serving pieces. Sprinkle with salt and pepper. Dip into egg mixture and roll in croutons. Place oil in shallow microwave dish. Microwave on HI for 3 minutes. Remove and arrange fish in dish. Cover and microwave on HI for 5 minutes or until fish flakes. Remove and drain fish. Serves 4.

HOT BROILED SHARK

2 pounds shark fillets
2 tablespoons vegetable oil
2 tablespoons soy sauce
2 tablespoons Worcestershire
  sauce

1 teaspoon paprika
½ teaspoon chili powder
½ teaspoon garlic powder
Tabasco sauce, dash

Cut fillets into serving size pieces. Lay skin side down in greased baking dish. Combine remaining ingredients and pour sauce over fillets. Broil 4 inches from heat for 15 minutes or until fish flakes. Baste with drippings occasionally. Garnish with lemon wedges.

MICROWAVE: Lay fillets skin side down in micro-dish. Combine remaining ingredients and pour sauce over fillets. Cover and cook on HI for 6 minutes or until fish flakes. Baste twice. Serves 4-6.

SHRIMP-KA-BOB

8 ounces shrimp, shelled
  & deveined
1 green pepper, chopped
¼ pound mushrooms
⅓ cup salad oil
¼ cup sauterne

¼ cup soy sauce
½ cup garlic clove, crushed
¼ teaspoon ginger
¼ teaspoon paprika
⅛ teaspoon pepper

Combine shrimp with remaining ingredients. Let marinate for 1 hour. Drain shrimp and thread on skewer. Alternate with onion, green pepper, and mushrooms. Broil 4-5 inches from heat for 4-5 minutes. Baste with marinade. Turn and broil an additional 4 minutes.

MICROWAVE: Combine shrimp with remaining ingredients. Let marinate for 1 hour. Drain shrimp and thread on wooden skewer. Alternate with onion, green pepper, and mushrooms. Microwave on HI for 6 minutes. Baste every two minutes. Serves 2.

SHRIMP-CRAB QUICHE

½ cup salad dressing
2 tablespoons self-rising flour
2 eggs, beaten
½ cup chablis
1 cup shrimp, cooked and
  deveined

1 6½-ounce can crab meat
1 cup Cheddar cheese, grated
½ cup celery, chopped
½ cup green onions, chopped
1 9-inch pastry shell

Preheat oven to 350 degrees. Combine salad dressing, flour, eggs and wine. Mix well. Stir in crab, shrimp, cheese, celery, and onion. Pour into pastry shell. Bake for 40 minutes.

MICROWAVE: Combine salad dressing, flour, eggs, and wine. Mix well. Stir in crab, shrimp, cheese, celery, and onion. Pour into pastry shell. Cook on HI for 10 minutes. Rotate dish ½ turn. Cook on HI for 5 additional minutes. Serves 6.

SHRIMP & VEGETABLES

2 tablespoons water
2 cups broccoli, chopped
1 cup celery, chopped
¼ cup green onion, sliced
1½ pounds shrimp, peeled
  & deveined
1 4-ounce can mushrooms,
  drained

⅛ teaspoon garlic powder
1 teaspoon salt
1 teaspoon instant chicken
  bouillon
1 cup boiling water
1 tablespoon cornstarch
1 tablespoon soy sauce

Add broccoli, celery, and green onion in casserole with water to cover. Cook at 350 degrees for 30 minutes. Add remaining ingredients and bake at 350 degrees for 20 minutes until sauce thickens.

MICROWAVE: Place water in 3-quart micro-casserole. Add vegetables and remaining ingredients, except cornstarch and soy sauce. Cover and micro-wave on HI for 5 minutes. Combine cornstarch and soy sauce and add to casserole. Microwave on HI for 3 minutes, until thickened. Stir half-way through. Serves 6.

SHRIMP NEWBURG

6 tablespoons butter or
  margarine
2 tablespoons flour
3 cups shrimp, cooked and
  cut up
1 teaspoon salt

⅛ teaspoon nutmeg
⅛ teaspoon paprika
3 tablespoons sherry
3 egg yolks, beaten
2 cups light cream
Toast cups

In 2-quart double-boiler, melt butter. Stir in flour, shrimp, nutmeg, paprika, salt, and sherry. Combine egg yolks and cream. Mix well. Stir yolk mixture into shrimp mixture. Cook over hot water. Stir until thickened. Serve over toast cups.

MICROWAVE: Soften butter. Blend in flour, cream, eggs, sherry, paprika, nutmeg, and salt. Cook covered on HI for 4 minutes in micro-dish. Add seafood and cook covered for 3 minutes. Serve over toast cups. Serves 6.

SHRIMP CALAIS

6 ounces mushrooms
1 tablespoon butter or
  margarine
6 cups rice, cooked
1 16-ounce can English peas
1 pound shrimp, cleaned &
  cooked

1 cup sour cream
½ cup milk
2 tablespoons lemon juice
1 teaspoon salt
1 cup croutons, crushed

Preheat oven to 375 degrees. Sauté mushrooms in butter. Mix mushrooms with remaining ingredients. Serve in seafood shells. Garnish with crushed croutons. Place in oven to brown crumbs.

MICROWAVE: In 1-quart micro-casserole, sauté mushrooms in butter for 3 minutes. Mix mushrooms with remaining ingredients. Scoop mixture into shells and garnish with crushed croutons. Serves 6.

SHRIMP CREOLE

⅓ cup vegetable oil
¼ cup flour
1 pound shrimp, cleaned & deveined
1 clove garlic, minced
2 tablespoons parsley
½ cup green pepper
1 cup water

2 teaspoons salt
½ teaspoon monosodium glutamate
½ teaspoon cayenne pepper
1 8-ounce can tomato sauce
1 8-ounce can Ro-tel tomatoes & green chilies

Place oil in skillet and heat at 350 degrees. Add flour and stir until brown. Lower heat and add shrimp. Cook 3 minutes. Add garlic, parsley, and green pepper, and cook 2 minutes. Raise heat and add remaining ingredients. Bring to a boil. Lower heat and simmer covered for 30 minutes. Serve over wild rice.

MICROWAVE: Place oil in 2-quart micro-casserole. Sauté garlic, parsley, and green pepper in oil for 3 minutes. Stir in flour after 1 minute. Add remaining ingredients, except shrimp. Cover and microwave on HI for 5 minutes. Add shrimp and microwave on HI for 3 minutes. Stir twice. Let stand 3 minutes. Serve over rice. Serves 4.

BARBECUED SHRIMP

4 pounds shrimp
½ pound butter or margarine
1 cup olive oil
1 8-ounce jar chili sauce
2½ tablespoons Worcestershire sauce
4 tablespoons lemon juice
2 tablespoons garlic salt

2 teaspoons parsley, chopped
2 teaspoons paprika
1 teaspoon cayenne pepper
1 teaspoon oregano
¼ teaspoon Tabasco sauce
1 teaspoon salt
½ teaspoon black pepper

Wash shrimp and place in large bowl. Put remaining ingredients in large pan and mix well over low heat. Pour over shrimp and refrigerate for 4 hours. Bake at 325 degrees for 30 minutes. Turn shrimp occasionally. Serve in soup or salad bowl with bread to dip in sauce.

MICROWAVE: Place shrimp in 3-quart microwave dish. Microwave butter in 2-cup measure for 2 minutes. Mix in remaining ingredients. Pour sauce over. Cover and cook on MEDIUM for 15 minutes. Stir occasionally. Let set for 3 minutes. Serve in soup or salad bowl with bread to dip in sauce. Serves 6-8.

POACHED RED SNAPPER

1½ cups hot water
⅓ cup chablis
2 peppercorns
1 lemon, sliced
1 bay leaf

1 teaspoon onion, minced
1 teaspoon salt
¼ teaspoon pepper
4 red snapper steaks,
  ½-inch thick

Place first 6 ingredients in fish poacher. Lower fish into poacher on rack and cover. Simmer for 15-20 minutes or until fish flakes. Remove and serve with your favorite sauce.

MICROWAVE: Place first 6 ingredients in 12 x 8-inch microwave baking dish. Cook on HI for 5 minutes. Place snapper in hot liquid. Cover and cook on HI for 1 minute. Let stand 4 minutes. Drain snapper and serve with sauce. Serves 4.

GRILLED RED SNAPPER

2 pounds red snapper fillets
½ cup melted butter or
  margarine
¼ cup lemon juice
2 teaspoons salt

¼ teaspoon white pepper
½ teaspoon Worcestershire
  sauce
Dash Tabasco sauce
⅛ teaspoon paprika

Place fillets on greased, hinged wire grill. Combine remaining ingredients except paprika. Brush sauce on fish and sprinkle with paprika. Cook 4 inches from coals for 8-10 minutes. Baste with sauce and sprinkle with paprika. Turn and cook additional 10 minutes or until fish flakes. Serves 6.

SMOKED SNAPPER

3 pounds (whole dressed) red
  snapper
1 quart water or 1 cup chablis,
  ¼ cup soy sauce & ¼ cup
  lemon juice

¼ cup salt
1 tablespoon tarragon
  leaves

Wash fish and set aside. Mix water and salt together in large dish. Add fish. Cover and marinate overnight in refrigerator. Remove fish and let drain for 30 minutes before smoking. Lay fish on greased grill. Add tarragon to water pan filled two-thirds full. Smoke for 3 hours or until fish flakes.

SNAPPER EN PAPILLOTE

2 pounds red snapper fillets
1¼ teaspoons paprika
2 teaspoons salt
⅛ teaspoon pepper
1 green pepper, sliced into rings

1 onion, sliced into rings
¼ cup butter or margarine,
**   melted**
2 tablespoons lemon juice

Preheat oven to 375 degrees. Brush fillets with half the butter. Sprinkle with seasonings. Lay cooking bag on baking dish and pour in remaining butter, lemon juice, green pepper, and onion. Lay fillets on top of vegetables. Close bag and punch holes in top. Bake for 25 minutes. Remove to platter. Garnish with cooked vegetables and serve.

MICROWAVE: Dot fillets with butter. Mix together remaining ingredients and place in micro-casserole. Lay fish on top. Cover. Cook 5 minutes on HI. Rotate dish half-way through. Let set 2 minutes. Serves 6.

SNAPPER FLORENTINE

2 10-ounce packages frozen
**   chopped spinach, thawed**
**   and liquid pressed out**
1 cup Cheddar cheese, diced
1 pound red snapper fillets
½ teaspoon salt

¼ teaspoon pepper
2 tablespoons salt & pepper
⅛ teaspoon oregano
¼ teaspoon lemon juice
2 tablespoons butter or
**   margarine**

Preheat oven to 375 degrees. Place a layer of spinach, cheese, and fish in shallow casserole. Sprinkle with salt and pepper. Add oregano, lemon juice, and dot with butter. Cover and bake for 30 minutes or until fish flakes easily.

MICROWAVE: Place spinach in shallow microwave dish. Cover and microwave on HI for 6 minutes. Press and drain liquid. Layer cheese and fish on top of spinach. Add seasonings. Cover and microwave on HI for 6 minutes or until fish flakes easily. Serves 4.

SOLE SWIRL

1½ pounds sole fillets
¼ teaspoon salt
⅛ teaspoon pepper
½ teaspoon Morton's Nature
  Seasonings
1½ teaspoons butter or
  margarine

1 cup mushrooms, chopped
1 tablespoon onion, minced
1 tablespoon soya flour
⅓ cup milk
⅓ cup mushroom soup
1 teaspoon parsley, chopped

Preheat oven to 400 degrees. Sprinkle fillets with salt, pepper, and seasonings. Cut fish into 8 1-inch strips and reserve remaining fish. Grease muffin tins. Roll fish strips and place one in each muffin cup. Chop remaining fish and set aside. Sauté mushrooms and onion in butter. Stir in soya flour and milk and mushroom soup. Stir until sauce thickens. Add chopped fish. Spoon mixture into tins and sprinkle with parsley. Bake for 20 minutes or until fish flakes easily. Remove from tins and serve.

MICROWAVE: Prepare fish as above and place strips in micro-proof muffin dish. Sauté mushrooms and onions in butter on HI for 2 minutes. Stir in soya flour, milk, and mushroom soup. Microwave on HI for 2 minutes. Stir half-way through. Add chopped fish. Spoon mixture into muffin dish and sprinkle with parsley. Microwave on HI for 5 minutes. Let set 2 minutes. Remove from muffin dish and serve. Serves 4.

SENSATIONAL SOLE

2 1-pound sole, skinned
2 tablespoons butter or
  margarine

1 teaspoon salt
¼ teaspoon pepper

Preheat oven to 350 degrees. Lay fish in shallow casserole. Dot with butter. Sprinkle with salt and pepper. Bake for 30 minutes or until fish flakes easily.

MICROWAVE: Lay fish side by side in shallow microwave dish. Dot with butter and sprinkle with salt and pepper. Cover and microwave on HI for 6 minutes. Rotate often. Serves 2-4.

FRIED SQUID

**1 pound squid tenacles,
  cut up
1 cup flour**

**2 eggs, beaten
1 cup bread crumbs**

Roll tenacle pieces in flour. Dip in egg and roll in bread crumbs. Deep fat fry until brown. Drain and serve. Serve with tartar or hollandaise sauce. Serves 6-8.

SWORDFISH SURPRISE

**1 pound swordfish steak
2 cups spinach, cooked and
  chopped
1 teaspoon orange rind, grated
1 clove garlic, minced**

**1 teaspoon anchovy paste
1 tablespoon parsley, chopped
½ teaspoon pepper
½ teaspoon allspice**

Preheat oven to 400 degrees. Cut steak into 2-inch squares. Place in broiler and cook for 2 minutes on each side. Drain spinach and place in saucepan. Add remaining ingredients. Cook for 10 minutes over low heat. Spoon mixture over fish squares and bake for 10 minutes.

MICROWAVE: Cut steak into 2-inch squares. Place in shallow casserole and microwave on HI for 2 minutes. Drain spinach and combine with remaining ingredients. Spoon mixture over fish squares. Microwave on HI for 3 minutes. Serves 2.

TUNA SURPRISE

1 7-ounce can tuna
½ teaspoon salt
1 teaspoon lemon juice
2 tablespoons salad dressing
¼ cup green pepper, chopped

⅛ teaspoon cayenne pepper
1 tablespoon butter or
  margarine
6 slices white bread
6 lemon slices

Mix together all ingredients except bread and lemon slices. Place mixture on bread slice. Broil for 10 minutes. Remove and garnish with lemon.

MICROWAVE: Mix together all ingredients except butter, white bread, and lemon slices. Remove the crusts from the bread and brush on butter. Cut slices in half. Arrange on oven shelf. Cook on HI for 1 minute. Scoop tuna mixture on each slice. Microwave on HI for 1 minute. Garnish with lemon slice. Serves 4.

TUNA FLORENTINE

1 10-ounce package frozen
  chopped spinach
3 tablespoons margarine
3 tablespoons all-purpose flour
1½ cups milk
1 chicken bouillon cube,
  crushed

2 tablespoons minced onion
½ teaspoon garlic powder
¼ cup shredded cheese
1 3-ounce can mushrooms
1 7-ounce can tuna

Cook spinach according to package directions; drain and set aside. Melt margarine over low heat; blend flour. Add milk, bouillon cube, onion, garlic powder, and cheese. Cook until thickened, stirring constantly. Add mushrooms and tuna. Mix well. Serve over spinach.

MICROWAVE: Cook spinach according to microwave instructions on package. Drain and set aside. Place butter in casserole and microwave on HI for 45 seconds. Blend in flour, 1 cup milk, bouillon cube, onion, and garlic powder. Microwave on HI for 2 minutes. Stir twice. Add cheese, mushrooms, and tuna. Mix well. Microwave on HI for 2 minutes. Serve over spinach. Serves 4.

TUNA TREAT

1 10¾-ounce can cream of
  mushroom soup
⅓ cup milk
2 cups peas, cooked and
  drained

1 7-ounce can tuna
2 eggs, separated
¼ cup Cheddar cheese,
  grated

Preheat oven to 400 degrees. Mix together soup, milk, and peas. Place flaked tuna in casserole. Pour soup mixture over tuna and toss. Bake for 12 minutes. Meanwhile separate eggs. Beat whites until fluffy; beat yolks until lemon-colored. Fold together and pour over tuna. Bake for an additional 20 minutes.

MICROWAVE: Mix together soup, milk, and peas. Place flaked tuna in micro-casserole. Pour soup mixture over tuna and toss. Cook on HI for 5 minutes. Meanwhile separate eggs. Beat whites until fluffy; beat yolks until lemon-colored. Fold together and pour over tuna. Cook on HI for an additional 4 minutes. Serves 2.

TUNA LOAF

2 7-ounce cans tuna
2 eggs
1 cup potato chips, crushed
1 10¼-ounce can cream of
  mushroom soup

½ cup celery, diced
¼ teaspoon salt
2 teaspoons lemon juice
1 tablespoon pimiento,
  chopped

Combine tuna, eggs, potato chips, cream of mushroom soup, celery, salt and lemon juice. Mix well. Pour into greased baking dish. Garnish with pimiento. Bake for 45 minutes or until firm in center. Remove from oven and let stand for 10 minutes. Remove from dish and slice.

MICROWAVE: Prepare loaf mixture as above. Place in micro-loaf dish. Microwave on HI for 9 minutes. Half-way through, rotate ½ turn. Let stand for 5 minutes. Remove from dish and slice. Serves 6.

TUNA CASSEROLE

½ cup onions, chopped
½ cup celery, chopped
1 8½-ounce can water
  chestnuts, chopped & drained
1 tablespoon vegetable oil
1 7-ounce can tuna, drained and
  flaked

2 tablespoons parsley, minced
1 10½-ounce can cream of
  celery soup
½ teaspoon curry powder
¼ cup light cream or milk
1 5-ounce can chow mein
  noodles

Sauté onion, celery, and water chestnuts in oil until onion is soft. Add tuna and parsley. Stir and continue to sauté for 1 minute. Combine soup, curry powder, cream and mix well. Pour in tuna mixture and add noodles. Reserve ½ cup noodles. Place mixture in shallow 1-quart casserole. Top with ½ cup noodles. Bake at 350 degrees for 45 minutes until crisp and lightly browned.

MICROWAVE: Place onion, celery, water chestnuts and oil in micro-casserole. Sauté on HI for 1 minute. Add tuna and parsley. Mix and sauté for 1 additional minute on HI. Add soup, curry powder, cream, ½ can noodles, and mix well. Sprinkle remaining noodles over top. Cook on HI for 4 minutes; rotate; and cook on HI for an additional 2 minutes. Serves 4.

TUNA-STUFFED PEPPERS

4 large green peppers
¼ cup butter or margarine,
  melted
1½ cups cracker crumbs
2 cups cheddar cheese, grated
3 6½-ounce cans tuna, flaked
  and drained

1 8-ounce can tomato sauce
¼ teaspoon salt
¼ teaspoon pepper
¼ teaspoon oregano

Parboil peppers in salted water for 4 minutes or until soft. Drain and dry. Pour butter over crumbs and mix well. Layer crumbs, cheese, and tuna in peppers. Top with cheese and tuna. Place sauce in small bowl and add seasonings. Pour ½ of sauce in bottom of casserole. Place peppers in casserole and bake at 350 degrees for 20 minutes. Baste with remaining sauce.

MICROWAVE: Steam peppers in steamer for 4 minutes or until soft. Pour butter over crumbs and mix well. Layer crumbs, cheese, and tuna in peppers. Top with cheese and tuna. Place sauce in small bowl and add seasonings. Pour ½ of sauce in bottom of micro-casserole. Place peppers in casserole and cook on HI for 4 minutes. Rotate half-way through. Baste with sauce. Serves 4.

WHALE LUAU

1 whale, medium
1 carload potatoes, chopped
1 carload carrots, chopped

Salt
Pepper

Cut whale into 1-inch squares. Takes 4 weeks. Add potatoes and carrots and place in 400 gallon pot. Cook 4 weeks at 350 degrees. Garnish with parsley. Serves 3,700. Salt and pepper to taste.

At this time no microwave is large enough to accommodate. If one is available, however, cooking time can be cut to 1 week on HI.

WHITING SURPRISE

1 pound whiting fillets
1 teaspoon shallots, chopped
1 teaspoon parsley, chopped
½ cup mushrooms, sliced
1 cup chablis

1 cup fish stock
1 cup Velouté sauce
1 tablespoon butter or
 margarine
1 tablespoon cheese, grated

Butter bottom of casserole. Sprinkle with shallots, parsley, and mushrooms. Lay fish on top. Add chablis and fish stock. Cover and bake for 30 minutes at 350 degrees. Drain half of liquid. Add Veloute sauce and butter to thicken. Baste fish and bake additional 10 minutes. Top with cheese and garnish with parsley.

MICROWAVE: Butter bottom of micro-dish. Sprinkle with shallots, parsley, and mushrooms. Lay fish on top. Add chablis and fish stock. Cook covered on MEDIUM for 2 minutes. Drain off half the liquid. Add Veloute sauce and butter. Baste whiting. Cook on HI for 45 seconds. Top with cheese. Heat on HI for 10 seconds to melt cheese. Garnish with parsley. Serves 2.

SWEETS

APPLE-MINCEMEAT FANTASY

2 cups mincemeat, prepared
½ teaspoon orange rind, grated
4 cups apples, cored, pared, sliced
¼ cup brown sugar
¼ cup instant non-fat dry milk
¼ cup oats, quick-cooking
⅛ teaspoon salt
½ teaspoon cinnamon
2 tablespoons butter or margarine, melted

Preheat oven to 350 degrees. Mix mincemeat, orange rind, and apples. Spread into greased 9 x 9 x 2-inch pan. Mix brown sugar, non-fat dry milk, oats, salt, and cinnamon. Add melted butter and mix until crumbly. Sprinkle over fruit mixture and bake for 45 minutes.

MICROWAVE: Mix ingredients as above. Use ungreased 9 x 9 x 2-inch micro-casserole. Microwave butter on HI for 30 seconds and pour over mixture. Blend well. Sprinkle over fruit mixture and microwave on BAKE for 10 minutes. Serves 8.

BROWNIES

⅓ cup butter or margarine,
  melted
1 cup sugar
2 teaspoons vanilla extract
2 eggs

½ cup all-purpose flour
⅓ cup cocoa
½ teaspoon salt
¾ cup pecans, chopped
¼ cup coconut, shredded

Combine butter and sugar and vanilla. Add eggs and beat well. Mix flour, cocoa, and salt. Add to butter mixture slowly. Stir in nuts and coconut. Pour into greased 9 x 9 x 1¾ inch baking pan. Bake at 350 degrees for 30 minutes. Cool and frost (see below).

MICROWAVE: Mix as above. Pour into greased 9 x 9 x 1¾ inch micro-dish. Microwave on HI for 7 minutes. Rotate dish half-way through. Cool and frost (see below).

CHOCOLATE FROSTING

⅛ cup shortening, melted
¼ cup cocoa
⅛ teaspoon salt

¼ cup milk
¾ teaspoon vanilla extract
1¾ cup confectioner's sugar

Combine all ingredients and blend until smooth. Serves 6.

CRANBERRY-APPLE DELIGHT

1 cup cranberry sauce
1 cup apples, pared and
  chopped
½ cup oatmeal, quick cooking
⅓ cup brown sugar

¼ teaspoon salt
3 tablespoons flour, all-purpose
3 tablespoons butter or
  margarine, melted
¼ cup pecans, chopped

Preheat oven to 350 degrees. Combine cranberry sauce and apple. Spread in greased 7 x 7 x 2-inch casserole. Mix together oatmeal, brown sugar, salt, and flour. Add butter and blend well. Sprinkle over fruit, then top with pecans. Bake for 1 hour.

MICROWAVE: Combine cranberry sauce and apples. Spread in 7 x 7 x 2-inch micro-casserole. Mix together oatmeal, brown sugar, salt, and flour. Microwave butter on HI for 30 seconds and add to mixture. Blend well. Sprinkle over fruit, then top with pecans. Microwave on HI for 10 minutes. Serves 6.

OATMEAL COOKIES

1 cup butter or margarine, melted	1¼ cups all-purpose flour
1 cup brown sugar	1 teaspoon soda
1 cup sugar	1 teaspoon salt
2 eggs, beaten	½ teaspoon cinnamon
1½ teaspoons vanilla extract	3 cups oatmeal
	1¾ cups pecans, chopped

Preheat oven to 350 degees. Combine all ingredients except oatmeal and nuts. Mix thoroughly. Add oatmeal and nuts gradually, until mixed. Roll in wax paper. Cut in ¼-inch slices. Place on greased cookie sheet and bake for 15 minutes.

MICROWAVE: Mix as above. Place on greased micro-cookie sheet. Micrwave on HI for 5 minutes. Makes 48 cookies.

QUICK N' EASY PIE

3 cups brown sugar	⅛ teaspoon salt
½ cup butter or margarine	1 teaspoon vanilla
3 eggs, beaten	1 9-inch pastry shell
½ cup whipping cream	

Preheat oven to 325 degrees. Combine sugar and margarine. Cream well. Add remaining ingredients except for pastry shell. Mix well and pour into shell. Bake for 45 minutes.

MICROWAVE: Combine sugar and margarine. Cream well. Add remaining ingredients, except for pastry shell. Mix well and pour into shell. Place in micro-pie dish and cook on BAKE for 10 minutes. Serves 6.

MARKET FORMS OF FISH

Whole fish

Drawn fish

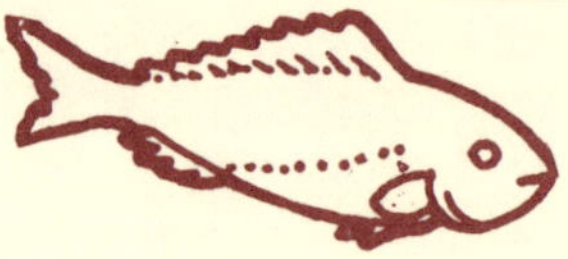

Dressed fish

Steaks

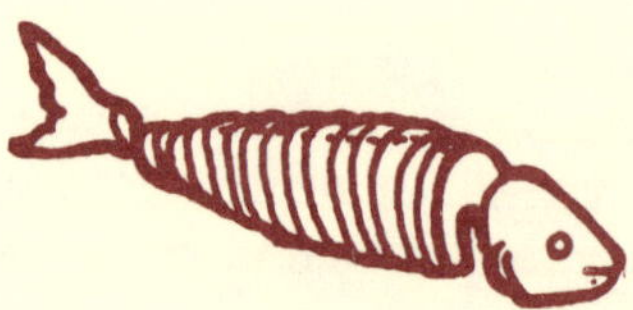

Fillets

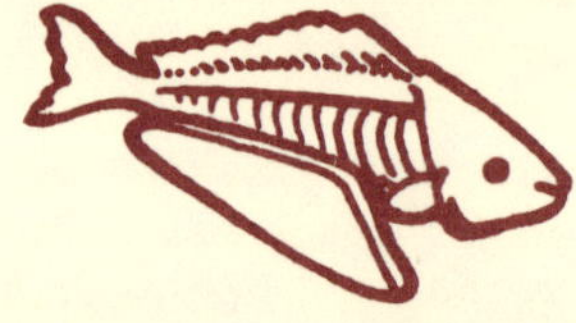

HOW TO FILLET FISH

1. Insert knife directly behind the gills. Cut down to bone, turn knife parallel to backbone, and cut down to tail.

2. Turn fish over and repeat this process.

3. After removing both fillets, remove rib section by cutting as close to rib-bone as possible.

4. Insert knife at tail section of each fillet and cut meat away from skin. Cut as close to skin as possible to save meat. Wash thoroughly.

5. The fillet is now ready for your preparation.

6. Cut the cheeks out on each side of the fish head. These are very tasty in soups and stews.

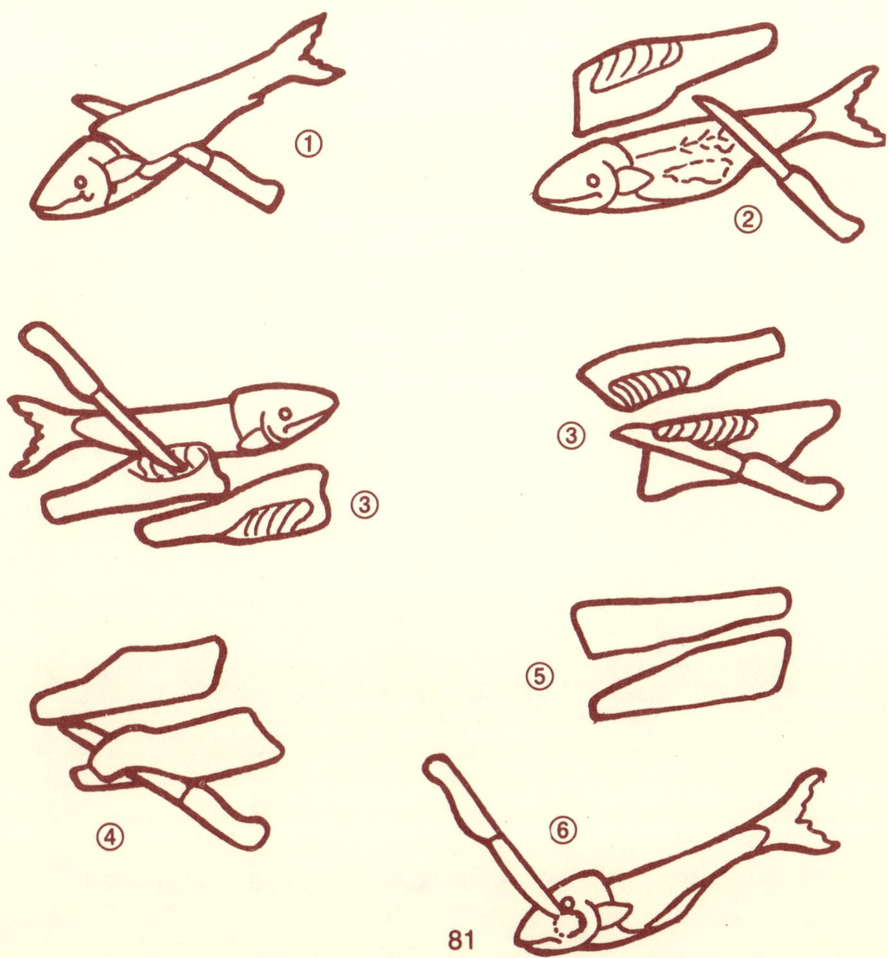

MENUS

MONDAY

LUNCH
Salmon Rolls
Kidney Bean Salad
Oyster Supreme Casserole
Pecan-Raisin Muffins

DINNER
Crab N' Crackers
Apricot Salad
Baked Apples
Light Muffins

TUESDAY

LUNCH
Roast Oysters
Crayfish Gumbo
Light Muffins or Crackers

DINNER
Clam Bake
Poached Crappie
Heavenly Salad

WEDNESDAY

LUNCH
Crab Stuffed Avocados
Baked Bass
Salmon Fruit Salad

DINNER
Sautéed Mushrooms
Shrimp-Crab Quiche
Broiled Peaches

THURSDAY

LUNCH
Trout Rolls
Tuna Casserole
Apricot Salad

DINNER
Oysters on the Half Shell
Bass Bouillabaisse
Apple-Mincemeat Fantasy

FRIDAY

LUNCH
Cheese N' Trout
Seafood Gumbo
Potato Salad
Pecan Raisin Muffins

DINNER
Crab Mornay
Barbecued Shrimp
Rockfish Salad
Banana Nut Bread

SATURDAY

LUNCH
Crab N' Crackers
Seafood Soup
Bass Burgers
Light Muffins

DINNER
Sautéed Mushrooms
Vinegar Cole Slaw
Mexican Hush Puppies
Southern Catfish Special
Fried Apple Rings
Quick N' Easy Pie

SUNDAY

LUNCH
Shrimp Stuffed Eggs
Zucchini Casserole
Scallop Salad
Tuna Loaf

DINNER
Tossed Salad
Trout Amandine
English Pea Casserole
Onion Bread
Cranberry-Apple Delight

INDEX

Limited edition prints by Jane Walker. These beautiful full color prints are signed and numbered by the artist. Send for yours today.

#101 Geese in Snowfield.
S/N 950. $42.50 each.*

#102 Greenheads in Flooded Woods.
S/N 950. $42.50 each.*

#103 Waterfowl Notecards.
10 assorted cards—10 envelopes
per box. $5.50 per box.*

*Includes postage and handling.